LE RUSSIE

SAVAGE LUXURY

THIS SPRING, AS IN EVERY SPRING, THERE WILL BEGIN ONE OF THE MOST BRUTAL ACTS EVER PERPE-
TRATED BY HUMANS AGAINST THE WILD KINGDOM. WE CALL IT...

THE MASSACRE OF THE SEALS

The perfect beauty of snow and ice against the brilliant blue of sea and sky, the utter silence, and
virgin purity in the Canadian Gulf of St. Lawrence provides one of the world's last glimpses of unspoiled
nature. In early spring the harp seal herd arrives to add life and meaning to the empty ice floes, and for a
few days the animals are at peace as the mother seals give birth. Then the hunters appear. For days they advance on the baby seals clubbing and kicking them to death. When they depart they leave behind thousands
of tiny carcasses, and blood-red ice. For too many years the seals have paid a terrible price for such a thing
as the luxurious sealskin round the shoulders of women far away.

The INTERNATIONAL FUND FOR ANIMAL WELFARE believes the bloody and careless killing of the
seals symbolizes man's total assault on his environment — an assault, motivated by base greed and compounded
by ignorance, that is fast becoming suicidal. We believe that what little is left of the world's wildlife and wild
places should be maintained in as natural a state as possible so that areas remain where man can renew
his own tired spirit.

The lovely and intelligent harp seals clustered on the sparkling ice floes in the spring of the year
are a unique example of nature in a brief but a recurring moment of breathtaking beauty. To destroy this is an
act of unparalleled barbarism.

We have worked hard for the seals giving of our best whenever opportunity was found, and we have
chieved some success. The hunt is now less cruel, and
wer seals killed annually in future years. But the que
t just how the seals are killed, or in what numbers, but

U.S. HELICOPTER PILOT RESTING NEAR DANANG
Enjoying the promised respite.

B &
1873

1923 Type 35 Bugatti

She BURNS

Leandre
Music
BMI

(Vocal)
J.O.Bryant

art I
ENDRICKS
S BAND
01

PARTY
ICE

229

BECK & AL HANSEN

PLAYING WITH MATCHES

PLUG IN

286 McDERMOT AVENUE
WINNIPEG, CANADA R3B 0T2
T. 204 942-1043 F. 204 944-8663
plugin@pangea.ca www.plugin.mb.ca

201 SAN VICENTE BLVD., #2
SANTA MONICA, CA 90402
T. 310 451-3867
waynewb@earthlink.net

DESIGN: WAYNE BAERWALDT AND SUSAN CHAFE
Editorial Assistance, Public Relations:
Susan Martin, Smart Art Press, Los Angeles

EXHIBITION SCHEDULE
MAY 9 - JULY 5, 1998
Santa Monica Museum of Art, Santa Monica, CA
SEPTEMBER 12 - OCTOBER 17, 1998
Thread Waxing Space, New York
NOVEMBER 14, 1998 - JANUARY 10, 1999
Plug In, Winnipeg, Canada

ISBN# 0-921381-13-1
Beck and Al Hansen: selected mixed media art including
collages, assemblages, video stills, photographs and texts.
Essays by Wayne Baerwaldt and Carlo McCormick.
Smart Reader Page text by Tom Patchett.

SMART ART PRESS

BERGAMOT STATION
2525 MICHIGAN AVENUE, BUILDING C1
SANTA MONICA, CALIFORNIA 90404
T. 310 264 4678
F. 310 264 4682
www.smartartpress.com

Distributed by RAM Publications
2525 Michigan Avenue
Santa Monica, CA 90404
T. 310 453-0043 F. 310 264-4888
rampub@gte.net

SMART ART PRESS
VOLUME IV, NO. 40

MADE IN CANADA

Foreground: Beck Hansen, Panic Button, 1997, mixed media, 30 x 18 x 3". Collection Bibbe Hansen and Sean Carrillo

TABLE OF **CONTENTS**

Image credits

Beck Hansen, Al Hansen, Charlie Gross, Bibbe Hansen,
Bill Short, Sean Carrillo, Dan Winters, Pietro Pellini, Yola Berbesz,
William Eakin, Sheila Spence, Hans-Hermann T., Wayne Baerwaldt,
Francesco Conz, Valerie Herouvis, Jan Van Raay, Michael Broome,
Gracie Mansion, Fabrizio Garghetti, Marion Morgenstern.

Cover: Al Hansen, Opium Venus, 1994, mixed media on poster board, 19¾ x 14".
Collection MRI Foundation, Milan/Genoa.
Inside Front Cover: Beck Hansen, Emergency Flag, 1998, mixed media, 31 x 24".
Collection of the artist. Photo on flap: Charlie Gross.
Inside Back Cover: Al Hansen, Untitled (Sketchbook, #1,246), mixed media, 17 x 14".
Collection Bibbe Hansen. Photo on flap: Francesco Conz, Verona.

Photo: Charlie Gross.

ON MY HEAD I TAKE THE RISK

WAYNE BAERWALDT

Between 1989 and 1991 the artist currently known as Beck Hansen made several trips to Cologne to see his grandfather, the Happenings intermedia artist Al Hansen. During this three-year period Beck and Al developed significant bodies of mixed media work, incorporating images, words and performative elements that reconfirmed their mutual interests in the artmaking strategies that Al had initiated in New York, Los Angeles and Europe in the 1960s and '70s. Their exchange began years earlier. Beck's formative years in Los Angeles were influenced by Al's informal exchange of ideas and notes on art, music and life, which acted as a catalyst for the development of their respective investigations. Their pursuit and sampling of the flotsam and jetsam in everyday life were already established. Each had mined the fractured, marginal interstices between and around art and music, suggesting very clearly that art and music are not separate entities in a media-saturated world and that the mixing and sampling of media constitute both subject matter and medium.[1] Until Al's premature death in 1995, he continued to revise and promote a conceptual framework to Beck in which all kinds of matter and activity could be labeled "art," not only objects, texts and ideas but also the *vitality* of the body, its actions and its documentation, a process associated with Marcel Duchamp, Pierre Molinier, Carolee Schneemann, the Viennese Aktionismus group, Urs Lüthi, Bruce Nauman and others. Within this framework the creative process never ends; a finished product may be rare. The artist's integrity, an ongoing concern for both Beck and Al Hansen, was further strengthened and resolved by adhering to a particularly European model of artmaking, a seven-day-a-week commitment to merging art and life.[2]

The intermedia conceptual framework that will be introduced in the following text (and in the accompanying interview by Carlo McCormick) first emerged in the pre-and- post-World War I eras of growing modernist and Dada experimentation and cross-disciplinary, progressive artmaking around the world. Al and many Fluxus artists of the 1960s continued a modernist strategy to dissolve the artificial separations that elevated art above life or vice versa. It was the limited progressive climate of the late 1950s and early 1960s that provided subcultures in the visual and literary arts an opportunity to confront and surpass the expressionistic and marginal avant-garde activities that dominated the 1950s. This climate of experimentation exposed artists and a developing mass media audi-

ence to repeated confrontations with formalist aesthetics, when the hybrid art forms of the visual and literary arts, high technology, and art-as-action gained limited acceptance but successfully upset the hegemony of the expressionistic trends. Many artists rejected the materialistic nature of cultural production at the time, opting for immaterial, temporal exercises (i.e., performative works) to break down barriers between notions of high and low art and between art and life itself. Art historian Kristine Stiles maintains "their [performance artists'] powerful declaration of the body as form and content insisted on the primacy of human subjects over objects." [3] In reaction to a relatively closed system, artists began to document, archive and co-sponsor hybrid art forms and publications that found widespread acceptance only among their peers at the time.

To Al, the circumvention of artistic categories and end zones also "guaranteed his freedom from attachments and obligations," [4] and, against all odds, led to the development of a refined, recognizable oeuvre. His oeuvre is at once a process-oriented art derived from (among other things) Pop Art's mass market infomania but is also specific to a Zen sensibility that recognizes and fosters awareness of the many layers of ambiguity that naturally undermine the certainty of knowledge. Early in his career Al applied the Japanese Zen teachings of *wabi-sabi* to his output and claimed, "Wabi-sabi is thought to be unexplainable, anti-rational, zen-like; one can only feel it. Wabi-sabi is the beauty of things

imperfect, impermanent, or incomplete." Similarly, Beck's process-dependent visual and audio work reflects elements of wabi-sabi in the collecting, sorting, deconstructing and re-presenting of ephemera, sampled or recycled images and sound fragments. The forthcoming text examines aspects of Al and Beck's separate but symbiotic relationships to artmaking. The text is similarly afflicted, tainted if you will, with wabi-sabi, a tentative deliberation on an artmaking process that is still unfolding, inclusive of its contradictions and elusive tangents. To characterize the artwork of Beck Hansen, it is necessary to return to the legacy of Al Hansen.

Al's Pop Art and Zen influenced impulses were first brought together under the umbrella of a new theatre movement known as Happenings, a type of "crazy theatre" Al co-founded in New York in the late 1950s under John Cage's influence. [5] These impulses achieved a form in the early 1960s with a characteristic mix of disciplines, existing genres of art, and new media to create an unpredictable expression. In retrospect a litany of monikers from that era are now used as a form of shorthand to characterize '60s experimentation in the New York artworld: Judson Church/Gallery/Dance Theatre, Allan Kaprow, Carolee Schneemann's *Meat Joy*, Andy Warhol and the Factory, Pop Art and on and on. These monikers are often misleading and minimize the importance of process and the nature of artistic experimentation that often eludes critical assessment and commercial packaging. A challenge to Abstract Expressionism was thriving in the guise of intense innovation. Al recounts

much later, in 1995, how Happenings are pure experimentation:

> One of the things John Cage taught was, that if you began to compose music, or paint, or make a dance, and you knew what the end product would be, then you were not experimenting. The new is found through experimenting. To experiment one sets out to do things without knowing what the end result will be. You must agree in advance. John always said, to accept whatever happens. So the end product is a "happening." This is exactly the way I did all my Happenings. Free form. No rehearsals. [6]

In 1965 Al published his now classic Something Else Press book on avant-garde Happenings, *A Primer of Happenings and Time/Space Art*, intending to define, once and for all, the structure and subtle nuances of his creative foundation in experimentation. His attachment to wabi-sabi largely prevented a definitive statement and he continued to revise his interpretations of Happenings until his death. The book introduces Al's relationship to Happenings in a circuitous series of project descriptions and pronouncements that aims to integrate art and life, similar to the European Dadaist doctrines and manifestos of the 1915-20 period. Before Al died he revisited aspects of Happenings in the form of a handwritten text that appears later in this book. The following "sample happening by Hansen," penned in 1965, is representative of a Happening's original fluid form, the application of the art form's basic structure (i.e., no

Photos: Charlie Gross.

rehearsals, no expectations of the results) set adrift amidst unknown, chance interactions with participating artists and/or audiences. It is as incomplete, imperfect and impermanent today as it was then.

Silver City for Andy Warhol

Situation form builds an integral. That is to say, whenever I see something painted silver, I think of Andy Warhol. For instance, the heavy bicycle delivery trucks outside Gristede's anywhere, building fronts painted silver, doors, doorways. Something that is silver or chromium does not invoke him. There is nothing of Andy in coins, faucets, car adornments.

A can of silver paint must be splashed outside on the floor. Silver City is a place where everything is either very slow or very fast. It is like a tableau; it has a very special kind of time. It is different the way a memorial or a plaque is different from a church or union meeting hall.
Ritual is inferred but not practiced.
Things are silver. Things become silver.
A girl lies in bed and writes a letter home. A girl dictates it to her. The bed is elevated and higher in back than in front in a stage prop way.
There may be dancers. There are projections.
A large form of a man is made with wood and cardboard. Hair is newspaper. Sunglasses...A giant Andy Warhol is made.
There are aircraft sounds, everyone is covered with news.
A couple has a conversation.   - 1963 [7]

Al's texts in *A Primer of Happenings and Time /Space Art* reveal a range of socio-political concerns that were seeping into the white-cube art world at the time: broad issues related to the "lousy education system," the omnipresent injustices of the period, the need for spiritual awareness. The combining of his disparate concepts of artmaking and a counter-cultural paradigm shift to create "art for the good of all" does not sound out of place in the late 1990s, when once again art doesn't have to be politically serious and humour is more effective than earnest protest. Al's often absurd, precise instructions in *A Primer...* are not always in opposition to Al's chaotic collages of the lowest common materials and assemblages of cast-off materials from the gutter. Al was adept at collecting and patching the media's psycho-social detritus and recombining the voices, movements and visual materials into a signature art form similar to his handwritten text. The following is another sample from *A Primer...* :

Al Hansen's State of the Onion Message

There is no plan for living; choices are classically subjective, irrational and emotional. Everything is by accident, an anarchous accident. My collage theater expresses this, springs from it, the images like beautiful mushroom machines springing from the mind-spore underground. A theater of contradiction and paradox, warmly absurd. And I feel my theater does not judge.

A throbbing, energy-full megalopolis as incredible as New York City requires its lousy educational system, traffic congestion, top heavy red tape government and graft. New York City is crammed to the gunnels with stock savvy, tax hip winners from everywhere, who don't do a thing about being made to carry the rest of the state on their backs.

Photos: Charlie Gross.

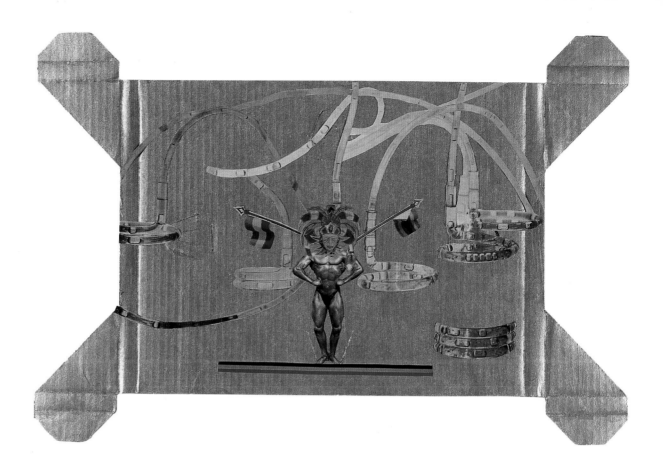

We thrive on crisis, corruption; the revolutions are piling up on each other. From the poorest individual unit of this great pachinko game called democracy to the largest GM-like corporate entities, all is for private profit rather than for the good of everybody. The rich get richer and the poor get poorer. The incredible thing is that so many desperately poor people are...content! This is probably the worst charge that can be made against education. They say we are in the midst of an information explosion and that over 80% of all recorded scientists are alive today! Fantastic?

Human history stems from the great sense of alienation from the natural order of the universe. Happenings, and indeed all other art, operate best in terms of an awareness of this natural order. This oneness is called, in Zen, satori. The causal mind considers the typical Zen hip parable as a nonsense joke. Rather than a rejection of reason, it is really a trip through the central process of reasoning.

I am interested in how things grow horns, tusks, fists, tress, conyons, national debts. My feeling about the happening is this: I would like to see the theater collage open and grow, blossom like a flower or a cabbage.[8]

Al's radar screen for interdisciplinary, intermedia art scanned far and wide for inspiration and an understanding of precedents for his Happenings process. The other major influence on Al's oeuvre (and subsequently Beck's) is Dada's late blossoming intermedia step-child, Fluxus, whose spirited manifesto of 1961 by Lithuanian immigrant ringleader, George Maciunas, claimed a plethora of mainly European, Japanese, Korean and North American converts in its anti-materialist sweep.[9] Al shirked the responsibility of full-time participation in Fluxus (or any other movement) but his contemporaries such as Nam June Paik, Joseph Beuys, Dick Higgins, Ben Patterson, Charlotte Moorman, Joe Jones, Alison Knowles, John Lennon, Yoko Ono and other international intermedia artists were recruited into the loosely knit group for varying periods of time. Fluxus actions, conceptual works and objects stretched the boundaries of art, incorporating elements of vaudevillian anarchy to prick the esoteric bubble of modernist abstraction. The blending of the visual and literary arts, new music/sound composition, performance art and theatre became a well-documented media event that propelled one of the last international avant-gardes of the 20th century. There are close but inconsistent similarities between Fluxus events and Al's

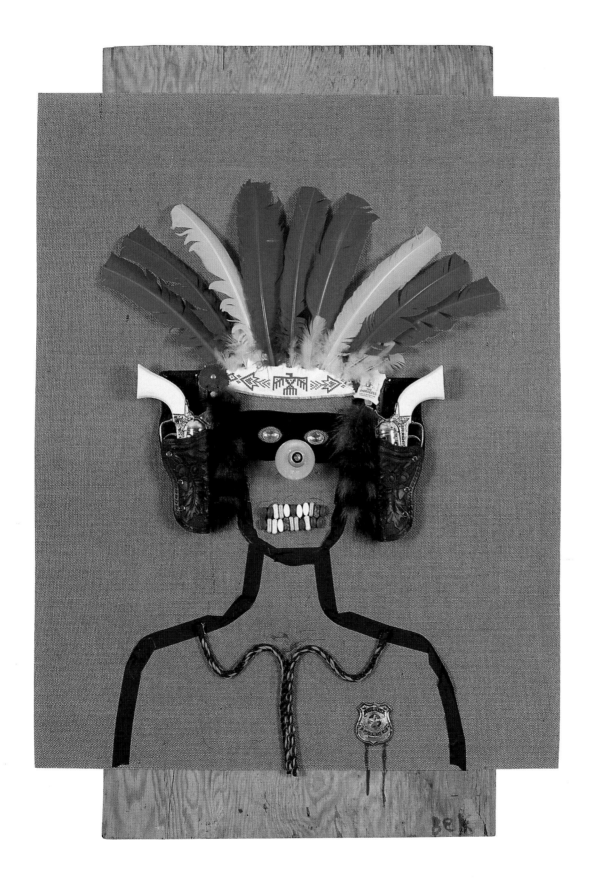

Ticket for the outpost shoutghost
Zoot suit trashwelder
Parachute revelator
Root digger
Bird thrower
Janitor vandal

Passage of bug ticket
For the matchstick traveller
Chaos beautician
With crankcase earwax
Greaselight thumbtacks
Half a moustache like a pirate broom

Hep-ho Al
Smokestack Al
Paper bag Al
Colorblind Al
Voodoo Al
My rocking horse guillotine
My backseat rhyme-master

"Pull down your pants and do the hot dog dance"

Shot pistol jazzes up their asses
My man Al revolving door spitting out holy debris
Dismantler of cankerous machinery

Fertilizer of barren lanes
Resurrector of phantom skins
Redeemer of disposables
Litter bug of escape hatches and back doors
Orchestrator of the moment movement.

One breathable intercourse
Constructor of invitations to the garbage life
The garbage moonlight
The garbage love

Digging on Al
Here's the letter I meant to sent
Here's the bent ticket and no more rent
Here's to you and your thing Al
Always Al
And always Al
And love to Al   *BECK HANSEN, JUNE 1995*
—

Photo: Charlie Gross.

brand of intermedia performance art and mixed media objects that deserve further explanation.

The first Wiesbaden Fluxorum festival in 1962 provided a stage for the often spare, minimalist form of performance that typified Fluxus activities. For example, Nam June Paik picked up a violin from a table and slowly raised it over his head until suddenly he swung it down onto the table, smashing it to pieces. This action, entitled *One for Violin Solo*, richly ambivalent, was deliberately composed for European and North American cultures burdened with the weight of Eurocentric importance. Another composition, *Piano Activities*, by American composer Philip Corner, consisted of the collective dismantling of a grand piano by the assembled artists onstage. These and other actions were part of a radical proposal to fuse and confuse the established categories of visual and literary art, art-as-action and music and, to some extent, to reveal the politics of their separations. The first of many Fluxus activities in 1962

exposed a means of deconstruction in multi-disciplinary artmaking that could fracture the traditional values and beliefs that protect and separate the classical arts from hybridization. Maciunas' Fluxus manifesto advocated "something flowing, something in motion, a continuing succession of changes...to promote living art." It is the infectious conviction that economical and easily distributed art represents an ongoing development of "successive changes." Like most Fluxus artists, Al coupled this notion with a focus on anti-art processes and an emphasis on the ephemeral, whose importance is being reassessed in the 1990s. Al's handwritten texts from the late 1980s and early '90s recap his earlier declared approaches to anti-art processes, in his particular case shaped by "a pattern of working, talking and research" not so different from the strategies of other Fluxus artists, except that styling, process and artmaking were, for Al, intimately linked, inseparable in the method that left an immaterial residue in his tracks.

The noted West Coast Happenings artist Allan Kaprow recounts:

> In the late 20th century of high-tech communications and multinational economics, the image of the wandering artist, the hobo avantgardist, seems anachronistic, if not self-conscious. Yet, Al Hansen cultivated the role - that's what it was - with great style and charm. It guaranteed him his freedom from attachments and obligations. He seemed to appear here and there and then vanish, leaving behind a gentle impression of easy friendship and vitality.[10]

It is this sense of Al's vitality, the ambiguous qualities that constitute presence and the lingering attributes of the personal in his absence, that anticipates a lexicon of languaging.

Vitality is, in effect, a subtle art action that charges the scraps of cloth and other material in a collage, the act of *cutting* paper, the *blowing* of cigarette *smoke* as a form of punctuation in an intermedia poem, the animated *chatter* in Al's collected telephone messages and performance video documentation. It allows the reading of a sensibility. Evidence of vitality resembles a stamp of presence situated somewhere between the material and immaterial, a form of languaging. It is a languaging that makes recognizable the unpredictable forms of an artist's work. Handwritten texts (as spoken-word intermedia poems), for example, are scattered throughout this book, bearing witness to an ill-defined presence in language. They are not simply personal notes to recount a life-sentence in artmaking, or inspiring resolutions to the lifelong mysteries of art's nebulous process. Al's language-based mixed media work did not stray from the challenge of both bearing testimony and establishing presence of bodily resonance in his absence. He understood this well. Up until his death Al continued to emphasize experimentation with Cage-influenced intermedia poems, gag-filled ephemera and an ego-driven, open format - often covering flat surfaces (paper, film, video) with a stream of consciousness

that Beck has also mastered in the 1990s. Beck and Al approach language and return to it, to reinvigorate the senses. The American writer Don DeLillo refers to this "affliction," suggesting as much about art-making strategies (seriality, thematic consistencies, signature materials, etc.) as the craftsmanship of writing, when he states:

> Language can be a form of counterhistory. The writer wants to construct a language that will be the book's life-giving force. He wants to submit to it. Let language shape the world. Let it break the faith of conventional re-creation. Language lives in everything it touches and it can be an agent of redemption, the thing that delivers us, paradoxically, from history's flat, thin tight and relentless designs, its arrange-ments of stark pages, and that allows us to find an unconstraining otherness, a free veer from time and place and fate.[11]

The links of both Al and Beck to the legacy of Fluxus are often tenuous and far from exclusive, as artistic intentions are highly idiosyncratic and peri-odically shift, veering in many directions from hith-erto predictable courses. Artistic strategies may embrace a language around experience and another around form. Their respective artwork is an aesthet-ic melange combining the irreverence and openness of Fluxus activity with a peculiar, dry, ready-made sensibility exemplified in their appropriation and sampling of materials. But ultimately, "in their mar-ginality lies their continuing power to fascinate."[12] Henry Martin, an art historian, writer, critic and

Fidel Castro looks out from the Concorde cockpit in Havana yesterday

long-time notary of things Fluxus, maintains that "Al Hansen was capable of seeing that the fertility of the notion of the Happening - the fertility of establishing a certain mode of intense but diffuse and shifting attention - lay partly in all the creative ways it might be misunderstood: 'Happenings have a reputation for being a great deal of energy and promise, [have] been misunderstood and and misinterpreted in wonderful ways....'"[13] Again, Happenings and Fluxus, both incredibly unstable, marginal (anti)movements, are purposely vague starting points for Al and Beck's broad repertoires. But they are consistently vague because Fluxus and Happenings artists often chose no particular forms; this legacy sustains what critic Barry Schwabsky has labeled "a quieter but more complex resonance" that aptly describes the richness of Beck's performative art and videos (i.e., *The New Pollution*) in the late 1990s.

Al purposely chose to distance himself from the mainstream art world later in life, to work the margins and maintain a highly idiosyncratic approach to selecting art materials and to employ a performative social dynamic that saw as much work made on the street and in bar rooms as in a studio. The results are so eclectic that the artmaking process, the performative, becomes the key element of consistency - language intimately tied to the working method. Beck remembers Al teaching him how to rhyme at the age of five, which to Beck amounted to a "formula for endless expression and fucking around" with language and sound that was, by extension, intrinsically linked to fucking around with a vast, unlimited array of raw materials for visual art. The leap of faith that bridges disparate sounds and materials was second nature to Al, and the freedom and spontaneity of Al's approach was instantly appealing to Beck.

Beck Hansen, Untitled (Castro), 1997, mixed media on paper, 14 3/8 x 10 3/4". Collection of the artist.

The associations of poetry to sculpture and other art forms are not always clear. Al aimed to interpret these associations, to ideally have audiences take for granted their integration and interchangability. It is the poetry in sound that frees Al's text pieces, for example, to become sculptures, forging an interplay between the immaterial and material worlds. Al described his leap of faith as lodged in organic, magical sources in art that mix prehistory religion with what Al called "warm vibrations… because art is still heavily involved with non-verbal feeling related to the magic beginnings." [14] The Dutch writer, Max Bruinsma, writing on sound, silence and technology, comes close to describing the expansive potential of Al's approach when he maintains: "Sound is our immaterial environment, just as undeniable as the material, the visible, and just as reticent, so long as we do not project meanings onto it." [15]

Rhyming, along with ecclectic approachs to merging sound and images (i.e., the tearing of paper, the burning of matches and cigarettes, talking and gesturing) are part of the process that informs Al's texts, actions and collages. A portion of this book comprises a collection of Al's handwritten and transcribed texts from the Al Hansen Archive that spans a range of subjects and forms, from stream-of-consciousness remembrances to performance notations and explanations (with number chains, as suggested at the beginning of his Happenings practices by John Cage), from notes on Happenings and Fluxus to Al's collections of titles for articles he would never write. These texts are important links to Al's process. In some cases they may resemble visual poetry in their strong rhythms and concrete messaging, but they are more complex and not so easily defined. They are slippery and incomplete, docking pods of wabi-sabi.

What Beck and Al share is an eclectic rummaging for common materials and a propensity for sampling and juxtaposing choice bits with a sensitivity to the "magic" in artmaking. The most recognizable, shared feature in this process is an economy of means. Their materials are predominantly refuse, the images, objects and sounds that most people throw away or ignore, considered too rudimentary, unsophisticated and often too insignificant for recycling. In unexpected combinations of subject matter and materials, their works tread a fine line between visual art objects and art as conceptual ideas. Al arranged junk and garbage into innumerable motifs and what he called "signature looks:" wave forms and stark, model towers constructed of burnt matches and glue, a robot of strategically positioned glue sticks and cigarette lighters, an endless stream of Hershey bar

wrapper Goddess Venuses, or collages made entirely of cigarette butts, glue and feathers. Other pieces are constructed of found advertising or porn images - humourous, sexy, political or irreverent images - that may or may not be combined with an assortment of cast-off materials such as trivial personal notes, old envelopes, shopping lists, empty matchbooks, German beer coasters and other refuse.

Beck's collages may consist of line drawings of skulls, cryptic portraits with Latin text outlining the links to human tactile and auditory skills, hand-held calculators, found magazine illustrations, colored feathers, shredded paper and manipulated photographs. They are simultaneously elegant, crafted visual messages and shorthand travel notes from an ongoing voyage through the flotsam and jetsam of the late 20th century. Like Al, Beck transforms the ordinary and often negative detritus of a commercial imagistic and consumer society, turning the detritus or fragments back in on themselves for closer examination, separating and reconfiguring edited bits of images (and audio) to better re-evaluate their contrived and often jarring beauty. Beck's ongoing work remains true to the feeling that nothing is beneath his notice, or, as Henry Martin has remarked about Fluxus artists in general, that just about everything is worth being looked at or listened to or toyed with. The simplicity of means, the occasionally crude cut-and-paste techniques and humorous biker world one-liners as subject matter, point to the complexities of primary human realities and levels of attention that are, after all, not simple or primary at all.

Al Hansen's work operates in several "isms" that are common currency to emerging pop media artists like Beck. Al claims early influences by John Cage's brand of minimalism and by Gestalt psychology and theory, to observe the interactions among elements of integrals - shape, colour and textures - in a picture commonly experienced by viewers in an unconscious manner. Al's apparently casual approach to artmaking is infused with his notions of Gestalt, connecting not only figure/field aesthetics but also the body, "the meaning-constructing agent of sentience and knowledge," so closely examined by Kristine Stiles.[16] Although modest in scale, the visual and language-based works of Beck and Al access a vast museum of the unconscious where time spreads out in all directions. While Al's performances were largely for small, art world audiences, Beck's art is further complicated by mass media communciations and a global audience that contemplates Beck's abstracted performative vitality in the intimate surroundings of a living room.

Bomb or BMW?

Beck is best known for his audio recordings such as "Loser," and reciting intermedia poems on television specials. More recently the audio recording *Odelay* seemed to best collapse his myriad forms - all forms exhibiting what *Village Voice* writer Ann Powers calls his "junkman's passion for discarded styles and stances." His performances and videos are laced with overlapping references to Happenings, body art, the "real" Blues, and the jumbled voices of a generation of shattered narratives. Beck exacts the potential in things imperfect, impermanent or incomplete and edits economically, with two turntables and a microphone - the audio equivalent of cut-and-paste collaging.

I've listened to Odelay dozens of times, and what lines stick in my mind? 'Goin' back to Houston, do the hotdog dance/ Goin' back to Houston, to get me some pants.' How, you might ask, could this amusing nonsense snippet represent the lyrics for 1997's best album? Not if they're taken literally, that's for sure. But as another xeroxed image in Beck's epic of non sequiturs, pasted inbetween... Beck's little rhyme becomes a recovered mumble from a long-dead bluesman, or an advertising slogan made poignant by the passage of time, or a snatch of overheard small talk that gets your imagination running overtime. It offers up all sorts of whimsical story possibilities. [17]

Writer Barry Henssler further describes Beck's "ingenious ability to mix old and new styles with ease," to contrive a familiarity for those intimate surroundings yet lace it with surprising twists and turns. He writes:

The first cut on Odelay, "Devil's Haircut," sports a guitar riff reminiscent of Terry and the Pirates' "I Can Only Give You Everything" and features Beck's stream-of-consciousness lyrical flow. The title of the first single, "Where It's At," is a skewed reference to the John Lee Hooker album *That's Where It's At*. The song boasts Jimmy Smith-style keyboards that would be right at home on a Blue Note record. The vocals, however, are run through a vocoder, giving them a retro-futuristic vibe more akin to an old-school Africa Bambaataa track. "Sissyneck," with its carnival-flavored organ line, possesses a lap steel chorus hook that recalls the spirit of Hank Williams with more honky-tonk authenticity than a million mullet-haired country

artists could ever hope to muster. "Derelict" sounds like Mike Millius covering an old Hoagy Carmichael number at a recreation center in the middle of nowhere. [18]

Beck claims the processing of his sound pieces is nearly "unconscious", and goes on to state "I think it's my gut reaction and I immediately need to dismantle anything too sharp or coordinated. Is it a desire to disrupt the clichés? Creating in a new place where clichés don't exist would seem to solve this, but does it?... I would like to let the art stand still and let the viewer/listener do the subverting." [19]

Beck recounts that Al's voice left a key, memorable "imprint" affecting his reliance on the unconscious, intuition and the listener. Beck describes Al:

[He was] a great talker on a vast network of "stuff." Elemental and mundane, his perpetual monologue seemed to be a simulcast of the decades from 1920 to the '90s. No part of his life cancelled out another part, he was always in tune with the whole aggregation of experiences he'd had. His view seemed to be as expansive as the massive stores of junk he accumulated anywhere he went. I think it was his way of digging what was happening around him, letting it take him and teach, burn him, feed him or leave him. [20]

Another recognizable, shared aspect of their art is scale. Most of the items are of a scale that would allow Beck and Al to wander as "hobo avant gardists," to be mobile. Again, the postcards, scraps of text torn from newspapers and magazines, beer coasters, matches and matchbook covers and so forth, are modest in scale. Nothing is larger than a *flag kite* by Al (see page 96).

One extraordinary body of work by Beck, a series of collages in a large, hard-cover album, is particularly striking and mirrors the dynamic themes and materials shared with Al. The indelible imprint of Beck, however, is obvious. The layered compositions of found magazine images, manipulated photobooth self-portraits, surface areas crawling with masking tape, bundles of burnt wooden matches, tourist postcards and other bits of ephemera have been torn apart, sampled and layered into the more than 30 riveting collages. A selection of these pieces is reproduced in the first half of *Playing With Matches.*

low and lonely

low and lonely, sad an blue
thinking only of little you
always trying to keep from crying,
I'm low and lonely over you

Do you miss me say you do
long to kiss me do you do, I'm so blue
do you long dear for my return dear
I'm low an lonely over you

low and lonely, weary too
you the only true love I knew
don't be long dear you know its wrong dear
I'm low an lonely over you

My hair in the wind, the sun on my face, with a Softail beneath me,

12 BI

Although Beck has been turning out innovative, insightful drawings and collages since childhood (his mother, Bibbe Hansen, knowingly encouraged him to develop what she saw as innate, raw talent), the collages from this period comprise a startling reflection on a symbiotic, lifelong relationship with Al. Glimpses of one of their trips to Prague and Naples can be found in the collections of ravaged postcards, scraps of old city maps, Czech playing cards, handwritten lyrics and notes, and other matter. The collages reveal a fascination with juxtaposing found text and images with a sensibility similar to Al's. Al's reputation as an artist's artist was based on his orientation to very social, dynamic exchanges in public places - often as an extension of the artmaking process, often in transit. The discussions he initiated in farflung bars and restaurants, even the aural and physical pauses apparent in the process of smoking are palpable, made three-dimensional in his handling of materials.

His exposés and reflections of art and life became embedded in his roughhewn assemblages of the detritus of everyday life. Al's unflagging curiosity, humour and unbridled optimism led him to patch together often disparate and "negative" byproducts (like cigarette butts and burnt matches) into a signature artmaking process. For Beck, this barrage of dynamic exchanges of visual and oral matter established a veritable prism of potential directions for his hybrid visual work and, in particular, his sample-laden audio and complex performative work.

Beck's art is a crossover hybrid of forms and styles incorporating the languaging of sound and visual poetry, performative styling elements from a scattered, intense sampling of hip hop, country and blue grass, '60s style-gourmets like French crooner Serge Gainsbourg, and the minimalist potential for something intangible, conceptual, perhaps even spiritual. He is a leading proponent of a generation of artists who move fluidly among media,

sampling and improvising as a byproduct, debasing the arcana of high art forms - relying on chance and probability, incorporating the residue of new technology and stripping information and objects of extraneous matter. It is a process of distilling sounds, actions and signs, searching for some form of essence that is palpable only because essence seems possible again. The writer-film-maker Chris Kraus sums up this notion of potential when she writes, "Synchronicity shudders faster than the speed of light around the world." [21]

There is a strong and obvious symbiosis in the artists' shared obsession with collecting and restructuring refuse (both sounds and objects) and the emphasis on experimentation, using all available materials. Beck openly credits his appropriationist strategies in artmaking and sound to Al. Al's cut-and-paste technique, his reverence for "negative" refuse such as cigarette butts and burnt matches, is once again current. Beck approaches his broadly based process of appropriation with an eye to recycling materials and ideas from other eras (1950s-90s)

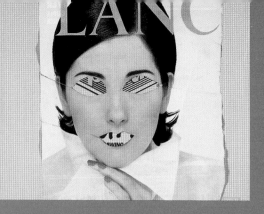

God speaks in sine waves of antique frequency. The universe lie factor remains, like a good story – good cos its not true. An inability to process truth lies in an inability to handle the pixels of circumstances; an awareness level reserved for minerals and bureaucrats.

These versions of waste are merely pictures embracing the lie, the alteration and rearrangement as a celebration of a vaporous game. We adjust the filter at will. The source subserves the culminative operation; ejaculations of an 8-way train. – *Beck Hansen*

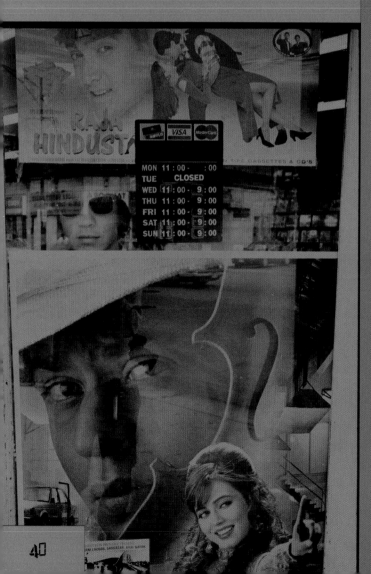

- what Al called flashbacks, remakes, replicas and replays - blending new life into them with touches of irony and a reverence for unidentifiable potential in materials that have become either formless or debased. It is a second sense at work, trusting intuition to blend sources into some unknown new entity. Al's influential collages from the early 1960s until his death in 1995 incorporate the artist's intuitive search for many of his recurring images and forms - big breasted Goddess Venus figures (see Al's homage text to the Goddess Venus), grids of performative photo-booth portraits and numerous found objects (such as Hershey bar wrappers, found text and images from magazine and newspaper sources) - these are similarly the raw materials for his videotaped art actions, sound poetry and assemblage sculptures.

Beck contributes a sense of wit and a wide-open pirating of images from sources as divergent as Tarot cards and mangled photographic self-portraits to still potent images of the low-down biker culture of southern California that has been the source of image bondage for bikers world-wide. The respective collages of Beck and Al share a range of free-wheeling, impulsive images and gestures, from bare-breasted women and bikers, drag racers, demonic self-portraits, grids of postcards and a world of collapsing meanings. The Hansens suggest that "there is a kind of terror or horrible boredom behind those supposedly inviting grins." [22]

Both artists have been inspired by experimental Happenings activities, Fluxus-style publications, stripped-down performance events of the 1960s and much later by sentimental hope and failure in the LA punk scene of the late '70s (Al managed the seminal punk group, the Screamers). Of interest in this book are examples of the initial markings by both artists, the base, often ugly, common things that reflect the chaotic drive of these formative movements and the individual gestures that set Al and Beck apart. The initial gestures are the elements that both artists elevate or transform, if not into something beautiful, then into something that is aesthetically interesting in its negative appeal. A lingering sense of failure is a constant in the pieces, underlining the sublime - that is, the terror and beauty in the works. In the late '90s Beck's anarchic stories/songs of lost love and dashed hopes are TV talk show staples and make failure a different sort of mass, experience that has lost its social stigma. The "junkyard vision of cultural life as hopeless" in the late '90s is not an end game but rather, a perfect regenerative starting point for the Hansens' shared mixed media language to unfold.

Q. Why don't you do beautiful art?

A. What I do is beautiful.

Q. How can junk be beautiful?

A. It comes from an ancient idea that God is in all things.

Q. Your art is a religious calling?

A. My art has left that behind.

Q. You feel there is no God?

A. Well, if we are talking about Him, He must exist.

Q. A lot of people argue there is no God.

A. That's kind of dumb to talk about Him and say He doesn't exist.

Q. Then you are a religious man.

A. In a way but I left it behind the way my art did.

Q. You worship junk and garbage?

A. No, I arrange it so it can be worshipped.

Q. You compose it like music?

A. Yes and I've made music of junk sounds.

Q. Random(ness) noise and chance sounds?

A. Yes, the flotsam and jetsam of life's sights and sounds.

Q. I don't think I would like to have your art on my walls or playing on my phonograph.

A. I assure you I can get along without you wanting it or liking it....[23]

END NOTES

[1] After an initial visit to Cologne in late 1969 for an exhibition called Happenings and Fluxus at the Cologne Kunstverein, Al came regularly to Europe until he finally settled in the city in 1980. From Cologne he made repeated jaunts to art fairs, gallerists and collectors between Copenhagen and Cairo. Wherever Al happened to be, he continued to produce an unending array of simple, often disarming works from the refuse of the streets and bars he frequented. Cigarette butts from bar ashtrays arranged according to filter tips, lipstick stains and length, beer coasters, wrappers and found magazine images all find their way into what he described as "negative impact" ephemeral pieces - "negative impact" being the kind of immediate reaction most viewers can imagine if they were to open Al's Suitcase Venus to an interior sculpted from dozens of filthy cigarette butts.

[2] See Al's intermedia poems, notes on artmaking, and letters from the Al Hansen Archive elsewhere in this book. Al repeatedly returned to the concepts that defined Fluxus, Happenings, new music and sound promoted by John Cage, as well as Body Art and other marginal art-related activity that often eluded definition or general acceptance as an artmaking technique or material.

[3] Kristine Stiles, "Performance Art," in Theories and Documents of Contemporary Art (Berkeley: University of California Press, 1996), 679.

[4] Allan Kaprow, "A Bit About Al Hansen" in Al Hansen Introspection (Köln: Kölnischer StadtMuseum, 1996), 183.

[5] Al participated in John Cage's music composition classes at the New School for Social Research in 1958, along with Allan Kaprow, George Brecht, Dick Higgins and others.

[6] Al Hansen, Oeuvre / Flashbacks (Rosenheim: Kunstverein Rosenheim, 1995), 54.

[7] Al Hansen, A Primer of Happenings and Time/Space Art (New York: Something Else Press, 1965), 125, 126.

[8] Ibid., 122-124.

[9] For an introduction to Fluxus see Wayne Baerwaldt, ed., Under the Influence of Fluxus (Winnipeg: Plug In Editions, 1991).

[10] Kaprow, 183.

[11] Don DeLillo, "The Moment the Cold War Began," from The Observer Review, January 4, 1998, 4.

[12] Barry Schwabsky, "Subject X: Notes on Performative Art," in Art/Text 60, 1998, 43.

[13] Henry Martin on Al Hansen, undated.

[14] Al Hansen in a note to Bibbe Hansen on the nature of artmaking, 1994.

[15] Max Bruinsma, "Notes of a Listener," from Sound by Artists (Banff: Walter Phillips Gallery, 1990), 88.

[16] See the selected writings of Kristine Stiles in the following: "Between Water and Stone: Fluxus Performance, A Metaphysics of Acts," in In the Spirit of Fluxus, (Minneapolis: Walker Art Center, 1994); Theories and Documents of Contemporary Art (Berkeley: University of California Press, 1996); "Uncorrupted Joy: International Art Actions," in Out of Actions (Los Angeles: MOCA, 1998).

[17] Ann Powers, "Babel On, Beck," Village Voice, Feb. 25, 1997, 11.

[18] Barry Henssler, 1996.

[19] Beck Hansen, in conversation with Jan Breslauer, Los Angeles, February, 1998.

[20] Ibid.

[21] Chris Kraus, I Love Dick (New York: Semiotext(e), 1997), 134.

[22] Al Hansen, undated letter (c. 1993-94) to Beck and Channing Hansen. Al Hansen Archive, Los Angeles.

[23] Al Hansen, Questions and Answers, Al Hansen Archive text, 1976.

Opposite: Beck Hansen, Get It, Girl!, 1990, mixed media, 12 x 12". Collection of the artist.

BIKEF

BIKER

IN THE EARLY SIXTIES I HAD HAD A SHOW OF HERSHEY'S CHOCOLATE WORD COLLAGES. IN THE MIDDLE SIXTIES I HAD A SHOW OF ~~KITE~~ SHAPED CANVASES ~~ANT~~ OF KITE SHAPES AND ROCKET SHIPS. I HAD BEEN PICKING UP OBJECTS FROM THE STREET AND FROM TRASH CANS THE SORT OF URBAN DETRITUS AND SCRAPS OF DECAY THAT KURT SCHWITTERS USED IN HIS COLLAGES. SCHWITTERS WAS VERY IMPORTANT TO ME ABOVE ALL HE WAS A MASTER COMPOSER, THE WAY HE PLACED OBJECTS IN RELATION TO EACH OTHER. I HAD SEVERAL BOXES AND PACKAGES OF THIS STUFF AND I DECIDED TO DO A SERIES OF COLLAGES EXPLORING THE POSSIBILITIES THAT WOULD COME UP. SO MUCH OF IT WAS SCHWITTERS LIKE MATERIAL THAT I DECIDED TO UNCOMPOSE IT; THAT IS INSTEAD OF COMPOSING AND MELDING THEM INTO UNIFIED WHOLES TO PUT THEM TOGETHER IN A WAY THAT JARRED, THAT MADE APPARENT THEY DID NOT GO TOGETHER. SO, IN A WAY, THEY WERE DECONSTRUCTED FROM A PROPER WAY TO CONSTRUCT OR COMPOSE THEM. THERE WERE LABELS, SEALS, TAGS, PICTURES OF TEETH, CANDY WRAPPERS, BOX ENDS, FEATHERS, CAPS, BOXTOPS, ETC. I BOUGHT A FEW DOZEN RAG BOARDS AND PROCEEDED TO TAKE OBJECTS OUT OF THE BOX AND FASTEN THEM DOWN I PUT THEM DOWN IN WAYS THAT THEY DID NOT GO TOGETHER. I ALSO DREW ON THE BOARDS. I BEGAN TO WORK ON FIVE, SIX, SEVEN OR TEN AT A TIME. I GOT A FEW 25 X 30 CM SKETCH BOOKS AND I WOULD GO THROUGH PASTING A DIFFERENT PIECE ON EACH PAGE. THEN I WOULD GO THROUGH ~~PASTING~~ GLUEING A SECOND SCRAP DOWN BUT NOT IN A WAY THAT IT HARMONIZED WITH PREVIOUS INTEGRALS.

Al Hansen

ROME: More than 100 Brazilian teenagers smashed up a Boeing 747 during a mid-flight riot on a trip from Sao Paolo to Rome, airport officials said today.

Crew on the Alitalia flight had to intervene to stop the 123 youths, aged 14 to 17, causing damage that would have risked the security of passengers, after the group went on the rampage two hours before landing.

The plane's captain called police when the plane touched down in Rome and the teenagers, who were stopping off in the Italian capital on their way to Tel Aviv in Israel, were charged with criminal damage.

78   52   29

Video still from The New Pollution. Directed by Beck Hansen, 1996.

I WILL DEAL WITH MY FILMS, VIDEOS, INSTALLATIONS PERFORMANCES, HAPPENINGS AND EVENT ART IN ANOTHER PLACE THIS IS AN INCOMPLETE OUT- LINE, RAMBLE, RAP OVER . . .

Al Hansen

L to R from top left, opposite page: 1-4. Al Hansen, Milano Poesia, Milan, 1989; 5. Al Hansen working, Cologne, 1992; 6. Al Hansen, Studio Morra II, Naples, 1988; 7. Al Hansen, Concert, Galerie Kolon, Cologne, 1992; 8,9. Al Hansen, Celebration Krieg, Urania Theatre, Cologne, 1995 (courtesy Yola Berbesz, Cologne); 10. Al Hansen, Muset for Santids Kunst Copenhagen, 1993, Video by Center for Videodocumentation; 11-13. Al Hansen and Hans-Hermann T., Vota Arte, Milan, 1994 (courtesy Lattuada Studio).

Above text courtesy Bibbe Hansen.

IN MY WRITING, IDEAS, PROJECTIONS, REMINISCENSES THINGS AND EVENTS FLOW ONE TO AND FROM ANOTHER. CONNECTIONS ARE RANDOM. THE SURFACE OR OUTSIDE SKIN OF A MUCH MORE COMPLEX AND SOPHISTIC-ATED UNDERNEATH WHICH I CAN CONTEMPLATE BEST IN SILENCE. THOUGHT. EVERYTHING BUMPS AND JOSTLES TOGETHER IN MY MIND SPACE, I SILENTLY AM AWARE OF UNDERLYING FREE ASSOCIATIONS BUT PICK WHICH STONES TO WALK ON AS PER THE CONVERSANT(S) THE PEOPLE I AM TALKING TO OR WITH.

I LIVE MORE AND MORE IN MY HEAD.

MY ART MY COLLAGES, PAINTINGS, ASSEMBLAGES, + PAINTINGS ARE DRAMATIC. I OPERATE ON THE SPECIFIC AND THE SYMBOLIC INTERFINGERED.

Left: Al Hansen, Miss Chicago, 1968, Hershey bar wrappers with paint on wood, 15 1/4 x 11 1/2". Collection Claes Oldenburg and Coosje Van Bruggen
Right: Photo: Hans-Hermann T., Cologne.

INTERVIEW WITH <u>BECK HANSEN</u>
by Carlo McCormick

In the arena of the obvious and overt that is popular culture, subtlety is lost, ambiguity or ambivalence is misread, process is obviated by product, and issues of identity are compressed into tokens of mass cultural membershipping. Smart pop is rare enough to be exceptional, but anything truly intelligent, elusive and subversive in pop music that can play on the debased stage of media spectacle is truly an anomaly. By these terms alone, Beck Hansen is remarkable. Perhaps it's genetic, maybe it's behavioral, or quite possibly it's environmental, but when one considers the multi-generational pedigree of unorthodox creativity and insouciant idiosyncrasy that runs in his family, all of a sudden the Fluxus poetics of grandpa Al, the transgressive pop and transgendered punk of mama Bibbe (and even the emerging artistic enigma of brother Channing) provide a fascinating context, if not explanation, for the less apparent motives and meanings invested in Beck's music. Articulating the self within the hegemony of consumerism, describing otherness to a culture of conformity, and still seeking the authentic, transformative, inventive and transgressive at the end of history that is this millennial malaise we live in, Beck has in many ways been able to distill the elusive essence of his lost generation by finding it in the aesthetic discourse of his grandfather Al Hansen's work. Maybe not essential to appreciating Beck's music, but certainly fruitful in terms of understanding it, is how he's applied the myriad strategies of experimental, conceptual and performance art to the populist realms of youth culture and the entertainment industry. Really smart without being in the least bit pretentious, best of all, he was both willing and able to talk about it.

I was hoping we could talk a little bit about Al, and more specifically how you may have adopted certain art strategies and applied them to pop music.

How it plays out in my thing is probably more subconscious, but I think a lot of it is genetic idiosyncrasies that probably go back to some fjord in Norway. There's a Viking element to our lineage. He was, you know, big on Norwegian mythology.

Yeah. Speaking of genetic idiosyncrasies, I know your brother Channing from when I was teaching at the San Francisco Art Institute. He's great.

Really? I didn't realise that. Channing does great work.

One thing I was thinking about was the use of serial images and repetition – how that's not only evident in Al's work, but in yours as well, from your collages to certain motifs that structure your songs.

Yeah, there are similarities. I think there's some fundamental kinship in how I approach what I do and however Al was operating - the desire and that need to reflect the dynamic of energy in art. That's the main thing I see in the collages. I think it's maybe more fundamentally an intuition beyond a convention or structure.

Would you say it's an improvisation method?

Yeah, but on the other hand it's very structured, and there's an invisible cognition here.

Al was a student of John Cage, so he was definitely aware of how the elements of chance and choice operate in the creative process. It seems to me, in that dichotomy between order and chaos, it is the chaotic in your work that best approximates the non-linear noise of popular culture.

Yeah, and I think Al recognized that too. His performance pieces were thematically chaotic.

Your music, and to maybe an even greater extent your videos, accumulate some wild and witty radical juxtapositions. What determines how and why such unlikely and disparate elements go together?

It has got to work on the most basic level. It has to make sense, even if only to me. It can't be totally intellectual. Whatever the idea, there has to be a pleasure in how these different things play off of each other. I try to work on that, and the more conceptual aspects will

ERYTHING YOU WANTED TO KNOW FROM UNDERWATER KNITTING
O VOMITING WITH DIGNITY...

Al Hansen

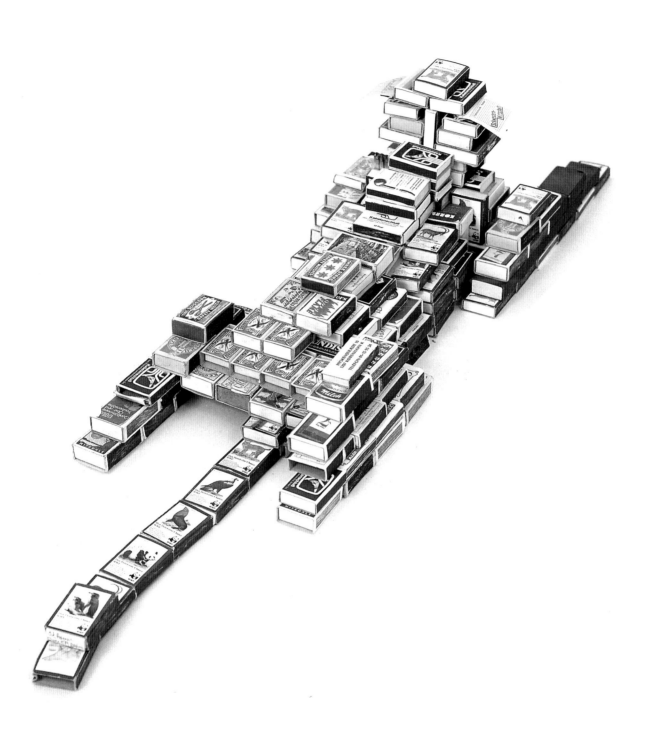

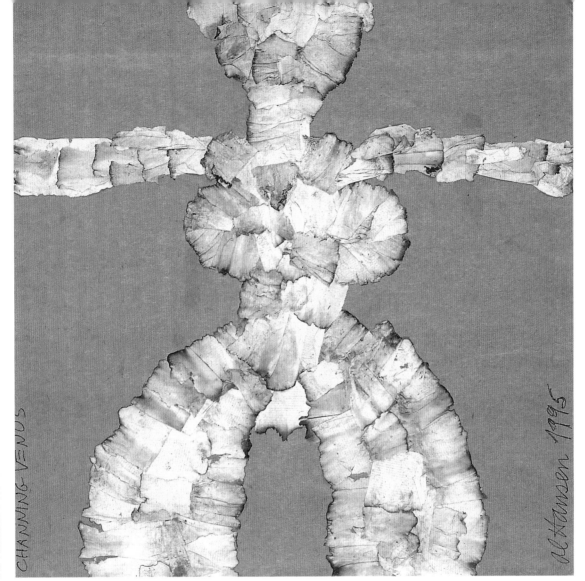

follow. There is often a lot of chaos in the studio. I'm sure when I mix things together there is a certain amount of chance involved that leads you to where you are supposed to be, that leads you to a somewhat final place where it all sticks together. But there is that tightrope act aspect to the whole process. And it's interesting to work with this in the context of the music business.

Where predictability is the formula for success.

Yeah, and just that the people who work in it aren't coming from an art background of chaos and chance, or if they are they don't codify it. So there is a certain amount of tension, and it really takes a lot of patience to push everything through when nobody knows where it is going. But I like that. I can work formally in a more struc-

tured singer/songwriter vein, but I'm really a lot more stimulated in the past five or six years just going in there with no preconceived ideas. I think it's the only way you're going to capture anything spontaneous and accidental. I like the awkwardness of the incidental. Sometimes my recordings really have that quality. I wish they could be more like Al where he'd look at one of his pieces, take a cigarette butt and glue it on, and it all looks like it's about to fall off. I have some pieces he did with pigeon feathers where over time they've all fallen off. And as I'm traveling around the world, occasionally I'll be walking around these streets, hanging out no where in particular, and see these odd collections of trash, with these pigeon feathers just like Al used. That was part of what he was trying to do. He'd be walking through

Madrid picking up pigeon feathers or whatever else no one cared about, and incorporating them into his art work.

Can you describe how that creative process works for you in the studio?

I tend to go in and pick up one instrument at random, see what happens, and go from there. I'll build it putting things end to end and over one another. I haven't formulated any tried and true process. It's definitely the mood. There are times when you struggle and have to get it together, and then there are times where everything flows, where there's a magic to it and you don't have to think about it.

Would you say it's a kind of assemblage?

I like to think of it as an orchestration. Just because when people tend to name something musical as assemblage or collage it cheapens it somehow. It kind of destroys the romance of the alchemy - the turning shit into gold. Besides, who says if you go in and use your $150,000 board, or if you're using a little $800 board, that's going to make it sound good or not. At that point it becomes an economic thing. From the '80s I was exposed to a whole marginal world of artists in LA, and learned to really appreciate the possibilities of low-fi. I feel when people take my music and say it's just collage or blenderized then it can't exist on the concourse with all the other work out there that's taken more seriously.

I love that notion of turning shit into gold. Perhaps it's pigeon feathers, or maybe it's cheesy '70s threads and line dancing, but whatever it is, that magic could never occur in the first place without a remarkably inclusive and democratic sensibility.

Well, yeah. After the fact, after the fact, after the fact. So it's not really democratic per se. It's democratic gone through 50 different incarnations and perversions of the idea of democratic, until we've ended up here. We live in a time where this sense of inclusion is presented as 'you are one of the select few who are hip to this thing' - culturally that is, but at the same time they're distributing it to everybody. I'm talking about the latest tennis shoe, or song; the latest product. There's a weird backwards democracy in that kind of thing. Everybody's an insider. Everybody's in the know, but it's not really okay to be a part of what everybody else is into. It sort of

moves it farther and farther away from what I'm attracted to in art or music.

Do you, or rather what you signify, feel somehow a part of that process?

No, I've operated a little around that. I've been victim of it a few times, you know, the issues of marketing. It's insidious, the fortuitousness of it.

It's more than the art of persuasion. It has come to be a ritual whereby youth now go to a succession of shops, from clothes to records, and literally buy their identity.

Exactly. It's really interesting in a scary sort of way.

Is this something you try to address, to subvert or fuck with in some way?

Yeah, you don't have to pretend to be into something that everyone else is into when you're not into it anymore. You can just go straight there and be on it. I don't know, maybe it's classism or something. Everybody has this desire to be a part of this select academy in the know.

Coming from such an art damaged family and ending up, well, a pop star of sorts, was there ever a conscious choice between say, academia, the avant-garde and commercial enterprise?

There was always a balance. I think it all came into play in terms of discerning what's valid. It's a very personal thing. I remember searching through the piles of junk and garbage in our garage in the mid-'70s when our grandfather moved out. It was just a mass of useless things. He'd have a pile of beautiful art book editions next to a stack of maybe 200 TV Guides. These things were equal in terms of some sort of neutered hierarchy - or not neutered, but maybe a hierarchy trapped in a fog bank.

Would you say you've tried to exercise that kind of populist democracy?

Definitely, because if you look at the art which to me has the greatest amount of friction and energy in it - art that is otherwise inherently static or inanimate - it has to have some sort of electricity to it, and that electricity is generated by the marriage of disparate elements. It belongs to some fundamental principle, like how colors go well together in a picture.

929

Or how some go really bad together in great ways.

Yeah, whatever.

In terms of such tensions, or frictions, how about the joke- the humorous aspects versus the serious?

It's so elemental, and it's what makes us not just pieces of meat walking around. It's essential to what's human- the soul. I find it interesting too that a lot of popular music is either total novelty joke or incredibly morose and personal. Certainly it can be both, but that's so rare. People don't really like to have it mixed up too much. They don't like the ambivalence of it.

Another very problematic ambivalence that plays into that is the precarious balance between irony and sincerity. Irony can be so cynical, but we can't be so completely sincere either anymore.

You can't be in the way that our great-great-grandfathers and grandmothers were. Because that, as something that once existed in the world, has been erased. But it is developing and hybridizing in other ways. We've stayed aware of it. It's still the big inspiration, the essence of meaning that we're looking for, much more so than humor is. Humor however, is I guess what our generation understands best.

Al certainly got it – I mean cigarette butts and Hersheys' wrappers!

Yeah, absolutely. He was very emphatic and over the top gesturing.

Also very much in relation to irony and sincerity is the position one now has to construct between innocence and knowing.

Yeah, I tend to try and not get too hung up on that. I'd

Above & opposite: Al Hansen, Why Shoot Andy Warhol? (details),1984, mixed media artist's book, original edition, 75 pages, 11 x 17³/₄". Photos: William Eakin. Collection Archive Conz, Verona.

EDGAR ALLEN POE INVENTED THE SPOOKY HORROR DETECTIVE STORY SOMETIME AFTER THE CIVIL WAR. IN INDUSTRIALIZING MID-1800'S AMERICA. THE INEXORABLE SEPERATION OF PEOPLE FROM NATURE WAS WELL UNDER WAY. MODERN SCHOOLS, ADVERTISING, DRUGS AND OIL WERE WELL UNDER WAY. BY THE 1870'S MY GRANDFATHER NICHOLAS ALFRED HANSEN WAS SAILING AS A CABIN BOY ON A BIG SCHOONER OUT OF LARVIK, NORWAY. HE SHIPPED OUT AT 14 YEARS. NOW 100 YEARS LATER SCIENCE AND INDUSTRY, FOR A FAT PAYCHECK HAVE CREATED SUCH A PILE OF SHIT, POLLUTION AND BAD IDEAS BETWEEN PEOPLE AND THE NATURE THAT THERE IS NO ENCHANTMENT LEFT IN THE WORLD. IF YOU HAVE ACCESS TO ENCHANTMENT AND NATURE, YOU ARE NOT ONLY AN UNUSUAL PERSON TODAY, YOU ARE ALSO VERY LUCKY. BUY A FLAK JACKET. DRINK BEER WITH YOUR BACK TO THE WALL, FACING THE DOOR. AT LEAST YOU WILL GET TO SEE THE MAD PERSON WHO WILL TRY TO KILL YOU FOR IT. EDGAR A. POE (USER) AND ROCKEFELLER (SELLER) WERE HEAVY INTO DOPE, OLD NICK

HANSEN SR. LIKED CIGARS, WHISKEY, BOATS AND WOMEN. I AM SURE THE ORDER CHANGED ACCORDING TO THE SOCIAL SITUATION. AMERICANS AND FOREIGN GUESTS WERE BUSY KILLING ALL THOSE BEAUTIFUL INDIANS WHO DIDN'T WANT THEIR LAND RAPED. EDGAR ALLEN POE 'WENT' TO WEST POINT, THE U.S. MILITARY ACADEMY UP THE HUDSON RIVER FROM SUNNY FUNNY OLD NEW YORK CITY. ABOUT THAT TIME MY 15 OR 16 YEAR OLD GRANDFATHER GOT FED UP WITH THE BRUTAL CAPTAIN OF THE SCHOONER AND ONE DARK NIGHT JUMPED SHIP IN PORT NEWARK NEW JERSEY, LITERATURE HAD 'CALLED' EDGAR ALLEN POE AND HE WAS WRITING HIS POEM ABOUT THE 'TINTINNABULATION OF THE BELLS BELLS, BELLS,' IN GREENWICH VILLAGE, INSPIRED BY CHURCH BELLS ON BROADWAY ABOVE 8 ST. WHERE ROBERT RAUSCHENBERG'S STUDIO OVER THE BILLIARD BALL SUPPLY CO. WAS. BOB AND STEVE PAXTON HAD A PET KOALA BEAR. DO NOT LISTEN TO QUANTAS, OZ'S DOWN UNDER AIRLINE COMMERCIALS ON TV. THOSE KOALAS ARE MEAN NASTY SUCKERS. A CLASSMATE

IN THE 1800'S THERE LIVED A FAMILY IN LOWER MANHATTAN WHO OWNED A LOT OF HOTELS. EACH HOTEL WAS NAMED FOR A SON. ALLAN KAPROW'S FAMILY OWNED HOTELS AND HE HAD A FEW OLDER BROTHERS WHO RUN THEM BUT THERE IS NO HOTEL ALLEN. ALBERT PINKHAM RYDER, A FAMOUS PAINTER AND A LONG TIME FAVORITE OF THE N.Y. SCHOOL. ENOUGH TO BE RON ONLY A FEW OF THE IN THE HOTEL ALBERT AFTER A FELLOW. MY GENERATION HAD GOOD FORTUNE TO THIS FAMILY AND CRAZY ART WORLD. MAKERS, POETS, ACTORS, WRITERS, SINGERS, ROCK BANDS BEGINNING TO MAKE IT STAY UP AT THE CHELSEA HOTEL ON W. 23RD. THE LOSERS THE DAMAGED AND THE MESSED UP ON THE WAY DOWN STAY IN HOTEL ALBERT ON UNIVERSITY PLACE IN THE VILLAGE OF MARK TWAIN, SAM COLT, MARCEL DUCHAMP, BIG WINNIE, PROFESSOR SEAGULL, AL HANSEN, BIBBE HANSEN, RONALD MAGER, FRANZ KLINE, YOKO ONO, AND WILDS CAROLEE SCHNEEMAN, JASON KOHN, MERCEDES MATTER, ETC ETC. CHELSEA & UPPERS. ALBERT IS DOWNERS. COKE IN THE PENTHOUSE, SMACK IN THE GHETTO. LIKE GEORGE BRECHT'S MULTIPLE, THE LIFE SENTENCE FOR SOME IS WEIGHTLESS, FOR OTHERS, SAY GIORDANO BRUNO IS VERY VERY HEAVY. ONE CAME BORN IN THE WRONG PERIOD. SOME LATE, SOME EARLY. BRUNO INVENTED THE HYDRAULIC JACK, A WAY TO USE FOCUSED PRESSURE TO LIFT MUCH LARGER

WEIGHTS THAN WAS KNOWN TO BE POSSIBLE WITH LEVERS, FULCRUMS + PRIZING. SHORTLY AFTER DEMONSTRATING HOW WELL IT WORKED HE WAS KILLED BY THE INQUISITION. ONLY VON SIRHAN WITH THE DEVIL COULD MAKE POSSIBLE SUCH INCREDIBLE LIFTING. HE WAS CRUSHED TO DEATH BY BIG ROCKS PLACED ON HIS CHEST ONE BY ONE. THAT WAS THE RENAISSANCE. SINCE TARTINI THE FORMED FANTASTIC VIOLIN WORKS SO IT WAS ASSUMED THAT HE WAS IN LEAGUE WITH THE DEVIL. SO ALL THE WOMEN SOUGHT TO MAKE LOVE WITH HIM. INDUSTRIALIZATION WAS UNDERWAY AND TO BE WRITE AN LP THAN A LIVE A YO YO LIFE ECONOMICALLY. WHEN FLUSH WITH FULL POCKETS I BECOME AN INTERESTING MIX OF ARROGANCE AND BENIGN DISPOSITION. SEVERAL TIMES, ATTEMPTING TO REBOUND FROM FINANCIAL DISASTER, I HAD TO HIT THE HOTEL ALBERT. IN THE MID-SIXTIES I LOST SEVERAL LOFT STUDIOS IN A ROW, AND WITH MY MAIN WOMAN, VALERIE HEROUVIS I MOVED INTO THE ALBERT. CROSSY BENJAMIN BRUCE THE JEWELER, COUNTESS PAULA ZANGI DI PRIMA, ALLAN MARLOWE, MADAME LUISA LESBIAN, RENE SECARD, MARGOT HOFFMAN, SUZY SNIFFERING, BOBBY FABULHASS, THE LIVING, POWERFUL HAD THE SUB BASEMENT. WE ALL KNEW EACH OTHER FROM HAUS KANSAS CITY. NAMED BY WEL OPPENHEIMER, THE FACEBALL TREE. MAX'S WAS REALLY A CITY AND WE ALL LIVED THERE. THE SIXTIES WERE WELL UNDER WAY. NIGHT AND VALERIE AND I WERE MAKING LOVE. BEAUTIFULLY.

IT IS GIVES US A FANTASTIC PUSH + THERE WE ARE, ALL FUCKED UP. 'WE'VE GOT TO GET THE BOOK DONE AS SOON AS POSSIBLE GERARD SAID' 'BABA BA BOOOOOM!' THE HEAVENS OPENED UP RAIN CAME DOWN LIKE CATS AND DOGS. SHIT WE RAN TO THE NEAREST SHOP AWNING. IT WAS A LUNCHEONETTE. ONE OF THOSE CANVAS THINGS GOING FROM STORE/DOORS TO THE STREET CURB SO RICH FOLKS WON'T GET WET. 'THEY ARE ALL IN NEW MEXICO', HETTY SAID. 'IRA COHEN HAS SOME,' I SAID. 'BUT HE NEVER GETS AROUND TO GIVING NE ONE, WHERE'S GEORGE BRECHT NOW,' ANGUS SAID. 'EUROPE, FRANCE, I THINK,' 'IRA WILL GIVE YOU A CALENDAR', HETTY SAID. THE RAIN KEPT COMING DOWN. WE WERE ON OUR WAY TO BE SHOT WITH ANDY BUT IT WAS RAINING TOO HARD. 'SHIT, LETS GO IN AND GET SOME COFFEE AND APPLE PIE,' I SAID. 'UNTIL THE RAIN STOPS, ITS GOING TO BE AWHILE.' WE WENT IN AND HAD COFFEE AND ANGUS AND HETTY TOLD THE HISTORY OF THEIR DRUG ENTRAPMENT BUST IN THE SOUTHWEST. VERY SIMILAR TO DR TIMOTHY LEARY'S. THEY DISCUSSED ASPECTS OF FIGHTING IT LEGALLY. 'WHY GO BACK TO HELL WITH THEM,' JOHN SAID. 'YEAH, BUT PEOPLE HAVE FORMED COMMITTEES AND ITS POLITICAL TOO, AND, AND, AND...' 'YEAH', I SAID. IT WAS LIKE TALKING TO CHRISTIAN MARTYRS BEFORE THEY WENT TO THE LIONS. 'HEY,' MALANGA SAID. IT STOPPED RAINING! WE PAID + GOT BACK ON THE STREET ONCE AGAIN. FIVE OF US ON THE WAY TO ANDY'S AT THIS VERY TIME MADNESS WAS IN THE SADDLE AT ANDY WARHOL'S FACTORY STUDIO, UP THERE BULLETS WERE FLYING

IT RAINED LIKE A COW PISSING ON A FLAT ROCK!

AS IT EXPLODED, THE WORLD EXPLODED WITH SOUNDS OF BIG PIECES OF GLASS FALLING AND BREAKING, SMASHING! THE WHOLE HOTEL SHOOK AS IF A GIANT SUBWAY TRAIN HAD GONE BELOW LIKE A HUGE HIDDEN DRUM UNDER THE CITY. WOMEN AND FAGGOTS SHRIEKING! IN THE STREET, YELLING CAR BRAKES, 'MY GOD! SHIT! OH LORDY!' THREE OR FOUR GROUPS CALLED IN AND CLAIMED THE EXPLOSION FROM THE 5 VIE CROATIA FRONT 'TO' PEACE TO'S UNLICENSED DOCTORS OF A MEDIUM HEIGHT. BUT THE PUERTO RICAN NATIONALIST TERRORIST ORGANIZATION DID IT TO THE VILLAGE VOICE NEWSPAPERS OFFICES A BLOCK NORTH. EVERYONE POURED OUT OF THE HOTEL HALF DRESSED TO HAVE A LOOK. GLASS LIKE CRYSTAL COVERED THE STREETS. IT WAS A SURREALIST WONDERLAND SCENE. I NOTICED VALERIE HAD PIECES OF SPSKA IN HER HAIR LIKE SEA FOAM FROM THE EXQUISITE BLOW JOB. THE SUPER CROZY POET, ANGUS MACLISE ONCE MADE A CALENDAR ASSIGNING MAD FREE TITLES FOR DIFFERENT DAYS OF THE YEAR. IT IS A FAVORITE ARTWORK OF GEORGE BRECHT AND I. I PARTICULARLY LIKED 'THE NIGHT OF THE BREAKING OF GREAT SHEETS OF GLASS.' AND NOW HERE IT WAS. THE EVENT WAS A MACLISE VALSE ME REENTERED THE HOTEL AND DRIFTED UP TO OUR ROOMS. THERE WAS A FUNNY TENSE MOOD IN THE HOTEL. BODY LANGUAGE. PEOPLE WERE GROUPED ATTENTIVELY OVER RADIOS AND TV SETS LIKE ORANGES IN OLD NEWS PHOTOS LISTENING TO RADIO SPEECHES BY CHURCHILL OR HITLER OR MUSSOLINI (DEPENDING ON WHAT

SIDE THE PEOPLE WHO RAN THE WORLD DECIDED YOU WOULD GET YOUR NEWS FROM.) WE REGULARLY SHOT AND KILLED IMPORTANT PEOPLE IN AMERICA. SO WE HAVE DEVELOPED A PERSONAL PARTICULAR WAY WE STAND AND RUN IN THESE MOMENTS. 'LETS GO BACK TO BED,' VALERIE SUGGESTED. 'SOMETHING HEAVY HAS GONE DOWN' I SAID. IT IS A PERFECT PROOF OF AMERICA'S CREATIVE AND EXPRESSIVE SCHIZOPHRENIA THAT WE ARE QUITE HAPPY TO COMMUNICATE DEEPLY WITH NON-VERBAL SYMBOL WORDS WITHOUT EXCHANGING ANY INFORMATION AT ALL. LIFE AS A MERBIUS STRIP OF COMMERCIAL SENSES NON-ANNOUNCEMENTS, READ THE PARK'S TRIBUNE, TIME NEWS PEAK. LISTEN TO THE SOUND FAT SOUND PLASTIC WIND UP DISC JACKEY NEWSPEAK ON AM AND FM 500 RADIOS. WE WENT TO OUR ROOM. 'LETS GO TO BED,' VALERIE SAID SOFTLY. THE HALL WE HEARD THE REPORT THAT SOME SICK, ATTRACTIVE YOUTH, ANOTHER BOBBY KENNEDY IS SIAN MANWAH DEATH' ON THE SCENE. WE LISTENED FOR AWHILE TO HOW SIRHAN SIRHAN, SUPPOSEDLY SHOT BOBBY KENNEDY, DROPPED DEAD IN THE HEAD HEAD. THAT NIGHT, SOMEWHERE IN THE BOWELS OF NEW YORK VALERIE SOLANIS WAS ASSAINING TO HAVE PISTOLAS AND BULLETS DELIVERED SOMETIME AFTER BREAKFAST. SHE PLANNED TO DO THE SAME THING TO ANDY PADA WARHOL THAT SIRHAN SIRHAN HAD DONE TO BUBBLING BOBBY KENNEDY. MANSON WAS STILL COLLECTING DEFECTIVE RUNAWAY TEEN GIRLS AT SPAHNS RANCH IN CALIFORNIA. POLANSKI AND SHARON TATE HAD BEEN HAVING BEACH PARTY FUN AND DISCUSSING WITCHCRAFT WITH BOBBY KENNEDY AND HIS WIFE ON A CALIFORNIA BEACH THE WEEK BEFORE. RICHARD HOROWITZ WAS ARRIVING IN PARIS TO SHOOT THE ST. LAURENT COLLECTION.

AROUND LIKE THE GUNFIGHT AT THE O.K. CORRAL! VALERIE SOLANIS HAD A BLAZING PISTOL IN EACH HAND AND WAS HAVING A WONDERFUL TIME TRYING TO SHOOT EVERYBODY. SHE WAS HITTING ANDY THE MOST. UP IN THE FACTORY BULLETS WERE FLYING AND SOULS WERE FRYING AS HELTER SKELTER IN THE FORM OF A SKINNY CHEMISTRY MANIAC WITH A LOADED GUN IN EACH HAND GRINNED AND POINTED AND SHOT AND SMILED AND SHOT AND AIMED AND GIGGLED WITH GLEE AND SHOT. IN THE STREET THE AIR WAS FRESH AND SWEET THE WAY IT IS IN NEW YORK CITY WHEN A SUDDEN THUNDERSTORM POUNDS ALL THE GASOLINE POLLUTION SHIT SHELL DOWN THE SEWER FOR TEN MINUTES. ANDY HAD FIVE OR SIX BULLETS IN HIM NOW. RICHOCHETS HAD SCARED THE SHIT OUT OF AND DOWN THE LEGS OF A DOZEN PEOPLE IN THE STUDIO. NO LOUNGE LIZARD THINKS HE OR SHE WILL EVER HAVE TO PAY DUES. BUT THE CHICKENS HAD COME HOME TO ROOST UP AT ANDY'S. IT MUST HAVE BEEN AS WE CROSSED 14TH ST. THAT VALERIE WITH SMOKING PISTOLS WALTZED OVER TO THE ELEVATOR AND PUSHED THE DOWN BUTTON. ANDI'S STUDIO THERE IS A TYPICAL CONCRETE BUNKER FACTORY FLOOR WITH HEAVY FAT SUPPORTING COLUMNS. THE ENTOURAGE HAD BEEN DIVING AROUND THESE DUCKING THE FEMINIST FUSILLADE OF HOT LEAD. AS SHE APPROACHED THE ELEVATOR FRED HUGHES CONFUSED CAME AROUND A COLUMN, SAW HER AND FROZE. FRED IS A SORT OF ECONOMICS DOYEN MANAGER OF ANDY'S ENTERPRISES. 'MR. PURSE STRINGS,' 'I'M GOING TO SHOOT

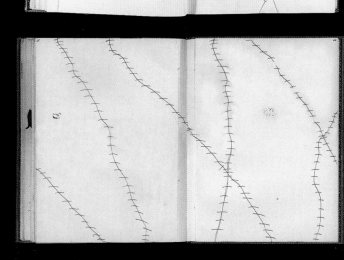

THE FLOOR WAS A LOVELY CAMPBELL'S TOMATO SOUP RED NOW..

rather get up on stage and cry and go for it rather than be too clever. I think we can have both, however. I guess it is more of a sordid era. It's a collection of references we all share, it's the common ground. But a lot of times I see people really enjoying tearing things apart. It's childish and not really looking at a bigger picture. You have to listen to what you're thinking, to your own voice.

If you would rather cry than be clever, how do all these elements, the personal and the social, come into play in that immense theatrical spectacle of your live concert performances?

When I'm crying, I meant tears of gratitude and hope. The beautiful sadness of it all, *Little House on the Prairie* style.

But showmanship is hardly incidental for you. At your level you've had to work on a much bigger canvas than Al had.

Yeah, but somehow it makes it more easy to be intimate. Because when I started out performing it was just myself and a guitar. It was this more intimate folk thing.

I remember you were a part of that "anti-folk" scene Latch organized at the Sidewalk Cafe here in New York.

Oh really, that must have been ten years ago now! That was a very different incarnation. Half of it would just be me talking. I loved it. You were right there with the audience. It was personal and I learned a lot about the nature of communicating with an audience at that time.

Folk, like most of the genres and styles you cite, is so referential to the broader canvas upon which the evolution of youth culture has been made evident in the age of leisure following the Second World War.

Sure, there's a lot of stuff in there, but I have a real problem with the notion that what I'm doing is retro. I'm definitely not into Retro.

What is your relationship to this collective cultural past then?

I'm not trying to recreate anything so much as sift through that common language to recontextualize and reinvent a new set of meanings. Like "The New Pollution" has a sort of '60s feel to it, but it's hybridized. We were going at totally sucking people into that whole Hullabaloo thing and then leaping into another thing.

One thing in relation to Retro is the incredible potency and prevalence of the past today. It's the power of history, which is really symptomatic of this particular fin-de-siècle period we're living in – which of course is also millennial. Any kid in the audience now, if you say '20s, '50s or '70s, they will conjure up a set of images. In five years however, just because of the arbitrary calendar we live by, you couldn't do that by saying '30s, you'd have to say 1930s – which would have little more meaning than 1830s really – because we'll all be looking forwards rather than backwards. It's a fundamental shift in perspective.

That's why I say the '60s through the '90s are going to be the same thing. It's all contemporary. It's all one blip.

Or even the '50s, which with the retrospective importance given to the Beats is very much a part of this post-war lineage of youth culture. I mean even Happy Days – is that '50s nostalgia now, or is it '70s television nostalgia?

I know. If you really think about it, what *Happy Days* was riffing on was only about 15 years after it happened. That was the beginning of that really quick turnaround of what is Retro. I think this really is the moment of the sound bite. I'm asked in interviews all the time- what is the crystallizing moment? What is your number one thing? The thing that can define everything. It's so closed minded, it's beyond narrow, it's just blindness. And that's something to break through, to get beyond. We've only accelerated this need to define and codify, to organize, separate, collate and stick into our Filofax all the appropriate and pertinent data.

To me one of the hardest questions your generation has to contend with – beyond even that whole mess of looking at things in generational terms – is that kind of sense of identity. When I was figuring out who I was as a kid I had Punk, just as the previous decades had their own dominant or underground movements to define themselves by. But by the '80s it started coming apart. I don't know, but I imagine of all the stupid questions you're asked again and again, one of the most common must be for you to speak for your generation.

That's for sure.

Al Hansen 1994

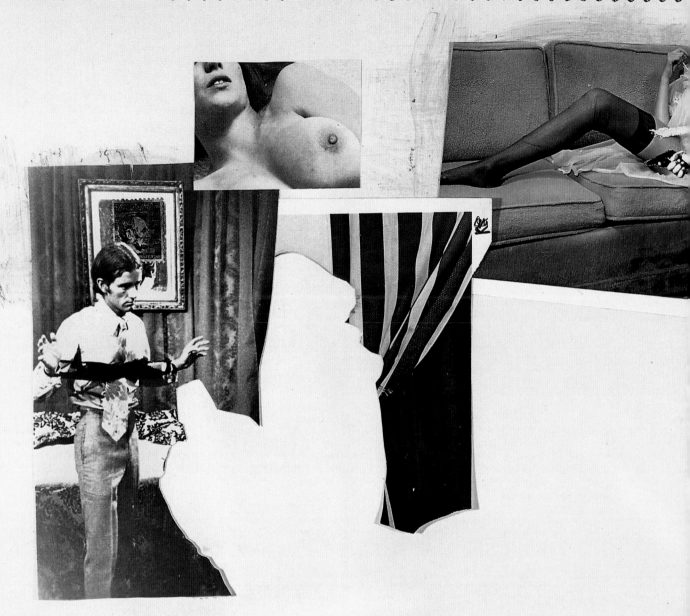

Al Hansen, Untitled (Sketchbook, #874), 1972, mixed media, 17 x 14". Collection Archive Conz, Verona.

"Loser" was so anthemic for this loss of identity being felt by kids today it was probably inevitable that you would be focused on as a spokesperson for your generation.

Yeah, but something that's also symptomatic of my generation is that they hate to have anything pronounced for them. So that song was the anti-pronouncement, but at the same time an anti-pronouncement is a pronouncement - at least in terms of media theory as laid down by the forefathers of marketing. I think we are in a tenuous position because we are the in-between generation. There's so many more of our parents, and according to what I've read, there's going to be just as many more of our children. We're going to be this ether, not really quite air but another kind of atmosphere they're just sending up into the actual atmosphere where everything happens. I think it is also that we haven't been allowed to understand or articulate who we are because we stand in such a gigantic shadow, and anything that we come up with gets eaten up so quick there isn't that time for it to grow into anything. You're trying to play at something and all the food is ripped off before it's even ripe, and then the thing just withers and dies. I don't know if this is necessarily a bad thing. Music is being made and people are into it. It's hard to say, on the other hand people could look back 15 years from now and say these were the glory days.

Inevitably they will.

They will. Somebody will latch on to this period and say it never got better - it's just the cycle of things. But it is amazing how hung up on it we are. I have lots of friends who are totally hung up on how old people are - that time defines who you are, what you're worth and what you can give to them. We like to reference everything, and that's one of the necessities of flux; to step beyond that slightly, or to step back into it and take it apart, depending on how you look at it. There used to be a sense of being comfortable with where we're at, what we're seeing and what we're knowing. We've lost that meditative quality where we can live within that, and maybe that could be the reason why we're so apt to try to compartmentalize everything.

Right, like when you say how resistant your generation is to be defined, it still can't stop Madison Avenue ad executives from needing to create some demographic label for the market. So they call it Generation X, with "X" I guess standing for that unknown x-factor they can't otherwise identify and explain.

Yeah, or as my friend Steve says, he's petitioning to rename it Generation Barbecue. How can you define something like that? We don't share a mass ethic. We don't share any single set of priorities. There is no group. They dismantled the group in the '60s, so we're operating outside that system. In a way it's more divisive and more individual. I think there's certain platforms all operating together.

I wanted to ask you if there was a politics to what you're doing. I can't think of a really good way to ask it, but if you could maybe think about it in terms of an awareness rather than a polemical statement it might make sense.

There is always a slight indication in what I'm doing of the perverseness of how we live and how our priorities are. I think I'm occupied with the predicament of our loss of ability to communicate to each other and to describe our experience. And somehow as a repercussion of that, our lack of understanding how to live, to enjoy or even experience a moment. But a lot of it I think are just the themes that have always been there and will always be there. A lot of my earlier songs were commenting more on feeling marginalized culturally and economically, with myself coming of age in the '80s one of these times of great prosperity, and not sharing in that - the invisibility of people like myself growing up. And what a revelation it was though when certain voices started to be heard. I thought it would never happen.

You mentioned in passing the perverse, and I'm curious about that, because there is an element of the perverse in your work, something undeniably pervy.

Yeah, we try to incorporate elements of what would be considered perverse by the puritans of our land who've proclaimed themselves righteous but have hidden their ignorance and intolerance under the canopy of that. So I wouldn't say it was perverse in the sense of exploiting others, but on stage we do try to get into some ambivalences about sexual ambiguity. White kids won't even deal with sexuality. There's hardly any sex within white

Top: Al Hansen, Song Slice, 1987, Hershey bar wrappers on wood, 11³/4 x 11³/4". Collection Bibbe Hansen.
Botton: Al Hansen, Lydia Orchidia, 1976, Hershey bar wrappers on wood, 5¹/4 x 9". Collection Bibbe Hansen.

alternative music. So I probably deal more with that in the art. A lot of the collages I've been working on deal with corporate culture and the obsession with physique and body perfection - how incredibly accepted these fascinations are, while they're ultimately the most perverse things. I think what I do on stage that would be construed as perverse is maybe perverse on stage, but in the realms of corporate life is considered completely the norm. We just try to engage in, well, you know the whole homo-erotic element of body-building and the muscle scene. But if you get up on stage, flounce around and thrust at your bass player, that's perverse.

You've also worked the ambivalent territories of androgyny.

Sure. There's also that point where the audience is about to be repelled but somehow they turn around and embrace it, and that's really satisfying.

Are you aware that you have a big following in the gay community?

I don't really know who my audience is, but it's really diverse. I remember when "Loser" came out, it was almost exclusively a white male frat-boy audience.

And you're singing about marginalization, that's kind of scary!

Yeah, it was very confrontational. I spent about a year performing, driving audiences out of rooms. And we garnered this reputation of being bad live. But actually in fact what we were doing was playing Spyro Gyra versions of our hits. We were trying to push the boundaries a bit, and there was a lot of performance art to it. But the audience has expanded since then, and I love them. They're incredibly tolerant and adventurous and fairly smart.

Yeah, I think people are pretty savvy to everything today. It's like nothing gets lost on them.

It's great. This is a good time, you can be a little more subtle.

Can you talk just generally about your relation to popular music today, like what you feel an affinity with.

Nothing that I would completely align myself to. But it is a time where you hear a song or two that you like.

You used to stay with John (Spencer) and Christina (Martinez) when you came to town. They were our downstairs neighbors for many years.

Top: Al Hansen, Venus of Shopritedorf, 1965, Shop-rite label collage on wood, 6³/4 x 13¹/2". Collection Idelle and Julian Weber.
Botton: Al Hansen, I Haven't Forgotten, 1967, Hershey bar wrapper venus collage on wood, 8¹/2 x 6¹/4". Collection Jasper Johns.

Oh really? Yeah, I was definitely influenced by Pussy Galore when I was a kid. I had Sonic Youth records and some other weird stuff. I listened to the Velvet Underground. When I got the *Right Now!* record it really turned me on. It was that music made out of garbage, a sensibility that really turned on some light bulbs.

We're really great at that trash aesthetic here, for obvious reasons.

Yeah, and that's where my grandfather comes from, so maybe it is predominantly a New York thing. Well, let me think, things I align myself with…it's pretty spread out.

Listening to your music, I imagine you have pretty eclectic tastes.

Yeah, I do. I don't usually like to give them away either, because people tend to just assume that I'm just ripping all those things off.

That's why I asked you to talk about it generally. To be honest I never write about those kinds of references or influences. I think it's a very lazy way to write about music.

It's so pervasive though. And it's harder to relate that inner life without it coming off too self-indulgent, ego-centric and self-centered. Or coming out too New Age, and a little too enlightened. So we've sort of opted to relating things to what's extraneous, and externalizing the internal. It's hard. I'm influenced by architecture. I'm influenced by my dining table as much as I am by the Beach Boys. But I think anybody else is too. There's noth-

ing idiosyncratic about that. I really appreciate what Bjork does. It is such a time of insane conservatism in music, though things are supposed to be expanding, and the drum and bass, and this and that, and that and this. Most of the other contemporary things I dig are coming from R & B and hip hop music, although I do get impatient by it because a lot of it's garbage. Anything spontaneous, completely natural and genuine usually comes from that territory of music. It seems like it gets incestuous there, like somebody copies something that copies something that copies somebody, until it comes all the way back around and it's fresh again.

I can see how that whole fluid process of continuous mutation would attract you however.

Yeah, it does. I think in pop music there's certain stones or markers that are unavoidable. There's this part of the minerals of the geology of how we operate and grow in music. That would be The Beatles, Neil Young, Dylan, Joni Mitchell, Sly Stone, James Brown, Aretha, David Bowie…everybody knows them. They're beyond being taken for granted. What can you possibly say about them that hasn't been said already? So you move from there and try to get into your own thing, your own life. But I'm not as concerned with things that are revelations, just things that are more contributions to the grander scheme - this thing that was set into motion so long ago. I mean how can we fool ourselves and pretend that we are some driving force to it. It's like there's a car going down the hill at sixty miles an hour, and you're just running along pretending you're pushing it. By all your efforts and might, you are some sort of martyr for the cause of keeping it moving. Well, it's moving and it's going to outpace all of us someday. And I'm going to step back and let some kids fuck it up and make it cooler than any of us ever did. That's just the cycle of things. But I'm getting a lot of people asking me where's it going? You know, this whole millennial thing is playing heavy. And it's like, who cares?

I've never cared much for speculating about the future, which none of us can predict anyway. I find I'm far more interested in how that uncertainty is effecting us today, and the way that that dynamic is getting even more dramatic and twisting things now is what makes this moment in time so incredibly interesting.

Yeah. I think of it as a perfume garden in the distance.

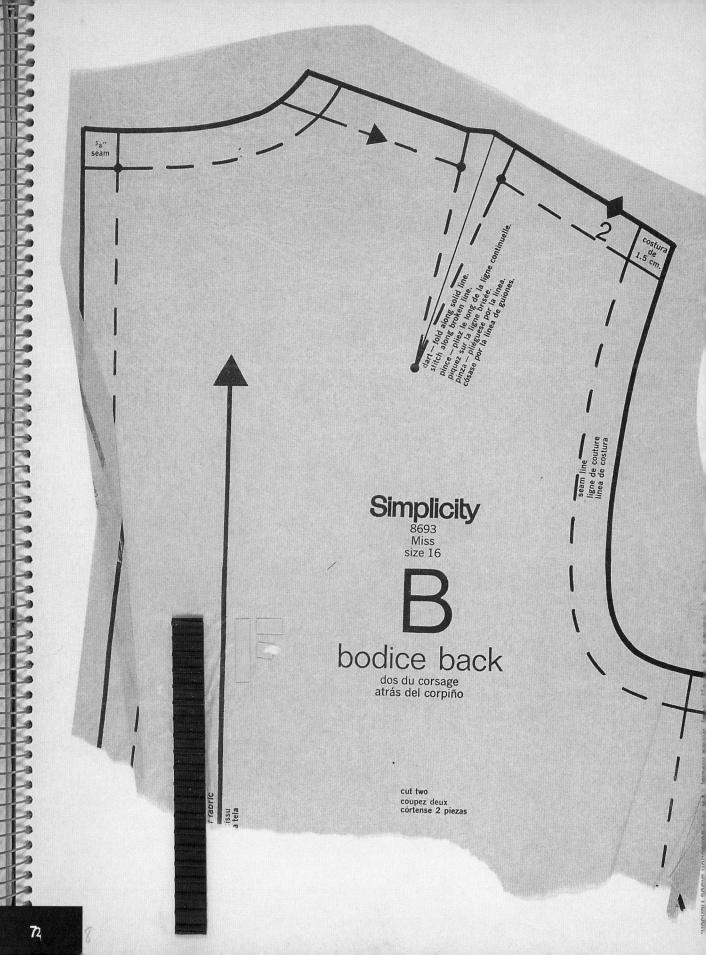

⅝″ seam

costura de 1.5 cm.

dart — fold along solid line.
stitch along broken line.
pince — pliez le long de la ligne continuelle.
piquez sur la ligne brisée.
pinza — pliéguese por la línea.
cósase por la línea de guiones.

seam line
ligne de couture
línea de costura

Simplicity
8693
Miss
size 16

B

bodice back
dos du corsage
atrás del corpiño

cut two
coupez deux
córtense 2 piezas

2

r fabric
issu
a tela

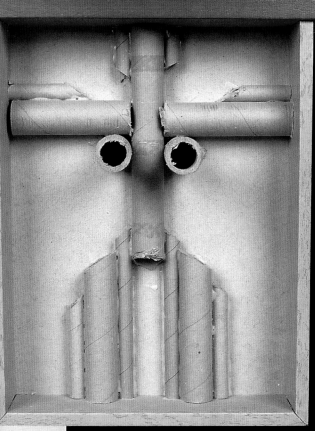

You always hear the wind chimes and smell the jasmine in the distance, but you never get to it. You never actually arrive there, it's always a promise.

Speaking of time, I've taken up enough of yours already. But before I let you go, I was reading some of your grandfather's writings and I thought maybe we could try two quotes of his out on you to see how closely you relate to them. The first is: "I see art as a magic act."

Yeah it is. Like anything creative, where you are drawing something extraordinary out of the ordinary, there is a magic there. It is a more elevated sense of magic. But I think there is something more in art beyond magic. I think it's fantastic, but everyone has a sense that they could do it themselves. They can see a piece of themselves in it. That's what attracts people to it. So it's more of a collaborative magic trick. But performing this magic trick, I do feel that there are certain things that are very simple, these little flourishes where you can always watch an audience go "ooooh…aaahh." There's something exhilarating in the cheapness of that thrill. But I like that quote. Al was very rough and tumble and hard, you know, sort of of-his-generation, and of his time and place. But he was also very romantic, and that's a romantic image.

Yeah, it gets to the heart of his poetics. And the other quote was: "It is my deeply felt belief that art making is a built-in, psycho-social cultural imperative."

I'd say word up. Yes, it is an imperative like breathing and eating. A culture without art is prison. I think there's something interesting in the corporate work ethic that implicitly believes, or says, that art and music are somehow superfluous. It doesn't build nations and it doesn't feed people, but it does something beyond that which is nearly as essential. It won't keep your body alive like bread and water would, but it will sustain you in another way much more extensively than we would ever think. Δ

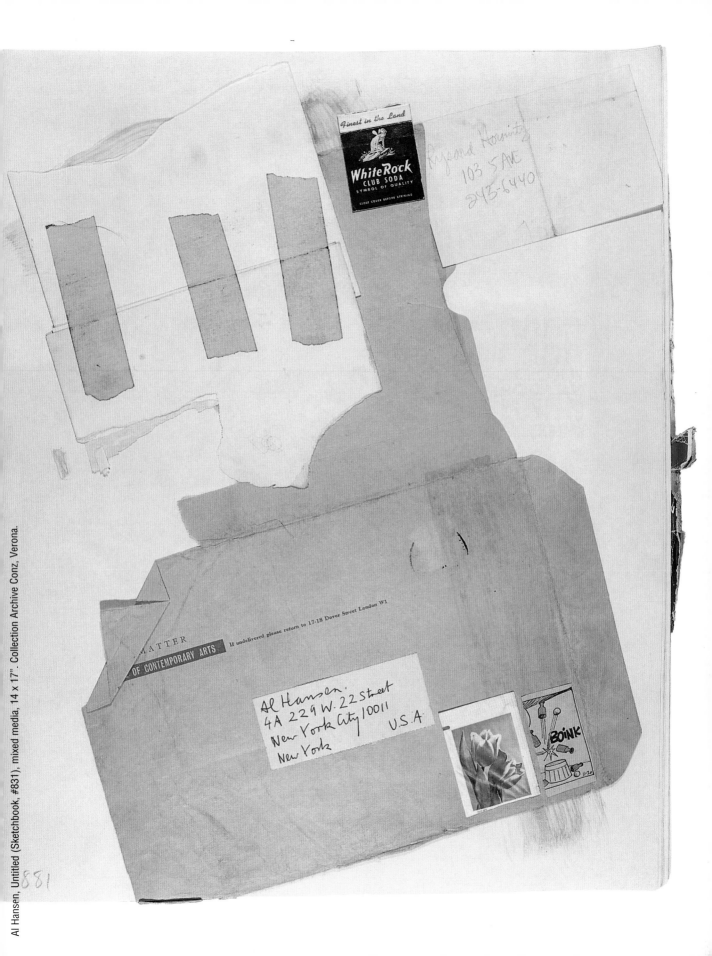

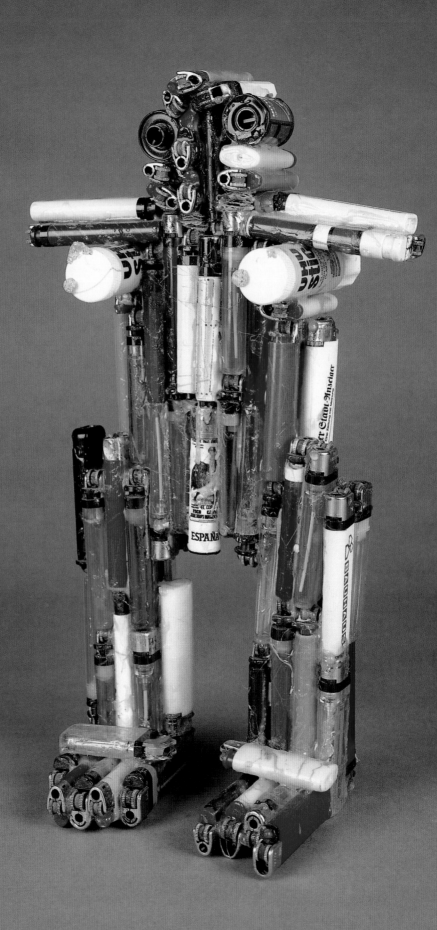

L & R: Al Hansen, Untitled (Sketchbooks, #1,627, #890 detail), mixed media, each 14x17". Collection Archive Conz, Verona.

Al Hansen, Nam June Robot, 1991, plastic lighters, glue sticks, glue, 12 x 3 x 5". Collection Bibbe Hansen.

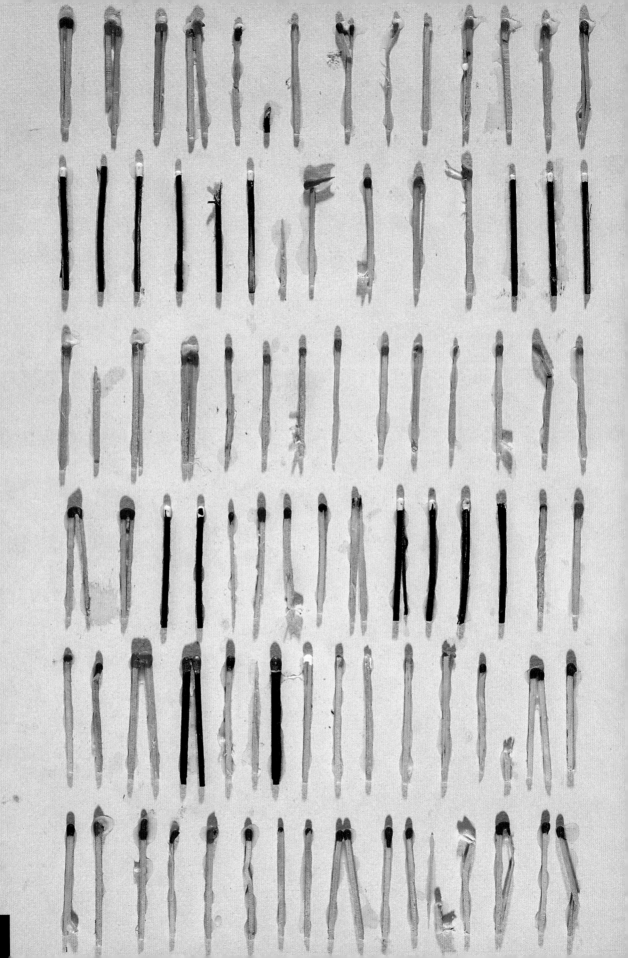

Al Hansen, Matches Museum (detail), 1993, wooden matches, glue on poster board, 10 ³/₄ x 17". Collection Bibbe Hansen.

AL HANSEN ON <u>FLUXUS</u>

Josef Beuys flew high in the sky, bombing and strafing in stukas and Heinkels. He crashed in the wilderness, was rescued from the wrecked plane and wrapped in felt by a Siberian Shaman. Beuys rose up from the dead as the democratic aesthetic conscience spirit of modern Germany.

Fluxus is a mini-encyclopedia of aesthetic alternatives. Concrete poetry - Found structures of text; surrealist dream combinations - of unusual objects and events; futuristic, strong actions and images; Dadaist sense from nonsense; Zen meaning through Anti-Art; Turn-of-the-Century "Art for Art's Sake" becoming Forties and Fifties Anti-Classical-Academic-Understood-Formal Art postures. These were all marinated together for the first half of the Twentieth Century. The psychodynamics of information build-up, demanded the cauldron of World War II. WWII could be seen to occur because of the threat to conservatism of information's increasing ability to disseminate itself - i.e.: Broadcasting.

Anyone who thinks Fluxus is serious misses the point. One who thinks Fluxus is not serious is closer to the point, but still misses the point. A unique thing about Fluxus is it is also not "in-between." Fluxus is not between "this" and "that." Fluxus is everywhere at once. And nowhere. It's secret is - it does not really exist - but it exists. In that way Fluxus is like God - it might not exist. But we talk about God and we talk about Fluxus.

Fluxus is healthy Anti-Art. Fluxus stretches to the breaking point the fabric of the known and accepted about art. One could say Fluxus is a "sui generis" cultural form. One could also say Fluxus was an "ultra generis" form. It is a rare, hard to identify flower in the world culture garden.

Rather more, Fluxus is a weed that will not go away. It was recently discovered that weeds take metals out of the earth. Experiments have shown that the cheapest way to reclaim metal solvent polluted land is to plant it with weeds.

Duchamp can be seen as a precursor to Fluxus. Puns are an important part of Fluxus. Word puns are Found language oddities. Puns and plays on words and unplayable music were important to Marcel Duchamp. As were Found ideas and Objects, multiples, and rubber stamps. Like Zen Buddhism and Groucho Marx dialogues, it is in the style of Fluxus to give quip-like, non-answers which usually seem facetious.

Yoko Ono works around the clock for more than a week preparing her Carnegie Hall Concert. She is very poor and has her apartment by being a building supervisor - cleaning halls and steps, attending to garbage cans, shoveling snow.

She ignores these tasks while working on her performance night preparations.

The performance night goes well.

She returns to the building focused on catching up with her work. It is about the time of Thanksgiving and Christmas. It is a big building. In the center is a garbage drop. People from all the apartments on each floor go to the little room and put their bags of garbage down the chute. In the cellar is a big furnace which burns it all to ash. But today it has gone out. One of her jobs was to keep it lit.

Now, back on the job, she lights it, not realizing the chute is packed solid with garbage. To the top floor solid. The fire in the furnace is fuel oil fed. The furnace itself is totally packed with garbage. The fire builds. The flames roar up through the garbage chute burning out the center of the building. Plumbing pipes melt. Water spurts and freezes. Electric wires fuse. Everyone is homeless including Yoko, her man Tony and their little daughter Kuriko. Where did more Fluxus happen? At Carnegie Recital Hall on 57th Street uptown? Or down on the cold streets with the guts of an apartment house burning out like an Icelandic volcano? People naked, wrapped in blankets, half dressed, half awake - half stoned, hopefully. Early sixties Fluxus? Happening?

Fluxus is a late night radio broadcast of three to five stations at once. Fluxus was the first all-out assault on intermedia areas and multi-aesthetic positionings, whereby an artwork spoke or operated under a broad range of aesthetic criteria.

Once in the old Cedar Bar, Franz Kline told me the only real abstract painting could be in your mid if you closed your eyes and someone whispered in your ear: "Four meters, lots of blue, a little red, big brush strokes." Kline said Fluxus is a phenomenon created by George Maciunas in such an effective way

that Fluxus can also be said to have created George Maciunas as well. A perfect chicken vs. the egg paradox.

Fluxus came about and grew through the mail, telephone calls, chance meetings in cafes, bars, buses, and trains. Fluxus was a deep sea net with holes in it. Fluxus is large, larger than Jon Hendricks and Siverman's would have American curators believe, but it is not all-inclusive. Many interesting fish were swimming elsewhere or sleeping on the bottom the years the Fluxus net went out. Not everyone who had access to "becoming" Fluxus did. Many had no access at all.

The Silverman Collection tries to have a very fine net with no holes. They limit Fluxus to only those objects which passed through Maciunas' hands. It's a bit like Helmut Kohl trying to limit the refugees pouring into Germany. "You have to draw a line somewhere!" say people with a bent towards strong discipline and control. The Silvermans have drawn a line around George's hands.

Politically, Maciunas was a fascist conservative. That the ideator-founder of such a curious little art movement (and a very radical one at that) could be a fascist who cheered when Rockefeller's National Guardsmen shot down the Attica convicts in revolutionary cold blood - well, it's fascinating.

Some people in contention for being Pre-Fluxus, Core Fluxus, For Fluxus, or Fluxus Relevant: Alison Knowles, George Brecht, Yoko Ono, Robert Filliou, Daniel Spoerri, Ben Vautier, Dick Higgins, Larry Poons, Geoff Hendricks, Laurie Anderson, Meredith Monk, Karl Valentin, Takako Saito, Joseph Beuys, Robin Page, Stanley Brown, Addi Kopcke, Nam June Paik, Stefan Wewerka, Emmet Williams, Ben Patterson, Ralston Farina, Pooh Kaye, Larry Miller, Myself, Claes Oldenburg, Bob Watts, Robert Smithson, Peter Hutchinson, Dorothy Iannone, Diter

Rot, Wolf Vostell, Kudo, Mark Brusse, Carolee Schneemann, Jan Van Raay, Barbara Heinisch, Urs Lüthi, Meret Oppenheim, Bob Rauschenberg, Allan Jones, Joan Semmel, Louise Nevelson, Sari Dienes, Jimmy Waring, Elizabeth Clarke, Christo Javacheff, Shigeku Kubota, Tajiri, Kosugi, Marcel Duchamp, Andy Warhol, Erro, Roy Lichtenstein, John Chamberlain, John Cage, Hiquily Ecker, Ray Johnson, Henning Christiansen, Ken Friedman, Chieko Shiomi, Tomas Schmidt, Albert Fine, Charlotte Moorman, Joe Jones.

There are so many names! One feels a nautilus shell opening and then there are twenty more names coming. The Vienna Aktionismus Group are important: Günter Brus, Hermann Nitsch, Otto Muehl, Osi Werner and relevant Viennese like Schwartzkogler, Cibulka, Valie Export and Peter Weibel. There's the Zaj Group of Spain - Juan Hildalgo. And Italians like Marchetti. And how could I leave out Jean-Jacques Lebel of France and Willem De Ridder of Holland? And there are more, many more. It makes quite an interesting puddle.

Trying to fit everyone into categories and placing them all correctly is impossible. At least for me. There is the "Old Guard" - Kaprow, Vostell, myself, Carolee Schneemann, Ray Johnson and Yoko Ono. At the Fluxus Exhibition at the Venice Biennale we were listed as "Pre-Fluxus." I liked that. I think Vostell, Yoko, and I overlap into Fluxus, but I'm not going to argue about it.

Most art movements march toward the blue chip, auction category with a proud shuffle. Fluxus artists are quite autistic, spastic; they do not fit in life and they do not fit easily into art. Even the art historians, aestheticians, gallerists, critics and art dealers who love them and make money from them have little idea what Fluxus is, how it works, or what it means. The strength of Fluxus is that - It doesn't matter! Fluxus is.

Fluxus is a One Man Show that got out of hand.

Fluxus was a crossbreed jackass that was impotent at reproducing young Fluxus artists.

Before beautiful Maciunas was born I was a young soldier in the army of occupation in Frankfurt/Main. Ein Falschirmspringer super soldaten. I was like a young firecracker looking for a match. 508th Parachute Infantry Regiment. Von Runstedt named us "The Red Devils." I don't think any other U.S. combat regiment was named by a German General. The 508 had the most medals and combat citations of any other American Unit in World War II.

We were billeted in Hedderheim, a suburb of Frankfurt. Our housing area covered many blocks where stray bombs had hit. The building next to my platoon was open to the sky. No roof. A pile of rubble in the basement. Going up stairs, if you opened the doors to the right, you entered apartments. To the left behind each door was the beginning of a room and a drop. Chairs, tables, pictures on the wall. A floor lamp. Sometimes the rug on the floor would hang a quarter meter into open space.

My squad on the platoon was on the top floor and through the door was such a Magritte scene. A room intact but open to the sky. Against the wall an upright piano stood. Above it a landscape picture. It was just a few centimeters from the edge. I thought about that piano standing on the top floor apartment so close to the edge of the four etage hole. I thought about it while drinking and eating. I thought about it while fucking. I thought about it while jumping out of airplanes, while shooting machine guns, while on guard duty.

March or so, 1946, Hedderheim Frankfurt/Main: One night I got ready for bed, stole up the stairs opened the door to the room on the stairs and the sky. I lifted the piano a bit and inched it toward the edge. The floor groaned. I dashed back. Then I tiptoed forward. Again I pushed it. Klonk! A bit went over the edge. The floor support beams creaked. I pushed it another few inches. The floor tilted a bit but held. I kept retreating to the doorway in case the floor suddenly gave way. I was a paratrooper - quick on my feet. Finally I got it to the point of no return. As it slid with a roar into the hole, I was through the door, dust wiped from my feet, and in bed with the covers pulled up playing "heavy sleeper." The sound that big oak piano made hitting? I still can hear it today: Tschwauuuuunnnngha!

It was wonderful.

Fourteen years later I returned to Germany for the Sohm Fluxus Happening show at the Köln Kunstverein. I wanted to push a piano off a high roof and record the sound of it hitting. This became "Yoko Ono Piano Drop."

Somehow pushing the piano off a high building seems to me to be Happening/Event Art.

And recording it and selling cassettes would be Fluxus.

Fluxus is like a chicken bone the world art dog cannot cough up. The way we saw it, Fluxus was always an "Open House," like a Saturday Night Fish Fry.

Fluxus is a Virtual Reality system where the glove doesn't work properly and the helmet doesn't fit. Other things happen than what was intended.

Scientists into bio-engineering are trying to put a flounder gene into a tomato to keep it from freezing. Sound like Fluxus?

"WHAT IS A HAPPENING?"

IN THE EARLY FIFTIES AT BLACK MOUNTAIN COLLEGE IN NORTH CAROLINA, M.C. RICHARDS HAD TRANSLATED <u>THE THEATER AND IT'S DOUBLE</u> BY ANTONIN ARTAUD (A FRENCH AVANT-GARDE THEATER PERSON) JOHN CAGE AND OTHERS GOT THE IDEA FROM ARTAUD THAT THEATER COULD TAKE PLACE FREE OF A TEXT, THAT IF A TEXT WERE IN IT, THAT IT NEED NOT DETERMINE THE OTHER ACTIONS, THAT SOUNDS THAT ACTIVITIES, AND SO FORTH COULD ALL BE FREE RATHER THAN TIED TOGETHER, SO THAT RATHER THAN THE DANCE EXPRESSING THE MUSIC, OR THE MUSIC EXPRESSING THE DANCE, THAT THE TWO COULD GO TOGETHER INDEPENDENTLY, NEITHER ONE CONTROLLING THE OTHER. AND THIS WAS DONE BY A GROUP OF ARTIST AT BLACK MOUNTAIN COLLEGE AND THE IDEA WAS EXTENDED NOT ONLY TO MUSIC AND DANCE; BUT TO POETRY AND PAINTING, AND SO FORTH, AND TO THE AUDIENCE. SO THAT THE AUDIENCE WAS NOT FOCUSED IN ONE PARTICULAR DIRECTION AS IT WOULD BE IN A THEATRE WITH A PROSCENIUM ARCH, A STAGE, CURTAINS, ETC. A WOMAN CAME EARLY AND ASKED JOHN CAGE WHERE THE BEST SEAT WAS AND HE SAID THEY WERE ALL EQUALLY GOOD BECAUSE THE SEATS FACED IN DIFFERENT DIRECTIONS AND THE DIFFERENT THINGS THAT WOULD HAPPEN WERE GOING TO HAPPEN IN THE AUDIENCE, AROUND IT, AND THROUGH IT.

WITH THE DEVELOPMENT, REALIZATION AND USE OF THESE IDEAS IN THE EARLY FIFTIES FORMAL NORMAL THEATER SEEMED TO BECOME PEDANTIC AND BANAL.

IN AMERICA THE BURGEONING OF MANY VARIETIES OF MODERN DANCE AS IT DIVERGED FROM CLASSICAL BALLET PROPOSED A TOTALLY NEW FORM OF THEATER. THUS, A THEATER WAS INDICATED THAT WOULD NOT USE ALL ITS MEANS TOWARD A LITERARY END SO A THEATER OTHER THAN THE ONE ARTAUD PROPOSED COULD DEVELOP. THIS WAS THE HAPPENING.

(THE ABOVE IS A CONDENSATION FROM SEVERAL CAGE INTERVIEW TEXTS.)

JOHN CAGE ONCE DEFINED EXPERIMENTATION TO ME AS A PROCESS WHERE WE SET OUT TO DO CERTAIN THINGS WITHOUT ANY IDEA WHAT THE RESULT WOULD BE. TO SET OUT TO DO OR PRESENT SOMETHING DECIDING IN ADVANCE TO ACCEPT WHATEVER THE PRODUCT OR END RESULT IS. SO THE END RESULT IS WHATEVER HAPPENS. THE HAPPENING.

HE ALSO SAID THAT WE GO TO THE THEATRE TO BE INSTRUCTED IN WHAT TO DO IN LIFE. ANCIENT GREEK THEATRE WAS TO INSTRUCT PEOPLE IN WHAT WOULD HAPPEN TO THEM IF THEY DIDN'T WORSHIP THE GODS PROPERLY. WITH A CLANKING OF CHAINS THE DEUS EX MACHINA WOULD COME DOWN, THE HUBRIS WOULD STRIKE.

THROUGH COMPOSING MUSIC BY USING CHANCE OPERATIONS LIKE ROLLING DICE OR THE I CHING JOHN CAGE FREED HIS WORK FROM PERSONAL CHOICES, HE SHORT CIRCUITED HIS EGO. HE DECONTROLLED HIS CONTROL OF IT. IT CAME INTO BEING FROM OUTSIDE HIS TASTE.

SO, IN ONE SENSE, THE PERFORMER PARTICIPANTS HAVE A LIST OF THINGS TO DO AND A GREAT DEAL OF FREEDOM OF CHOICE OF WHAT TO DO WHEN AND HOW. SO YOU HAVE WHAT COULD BE CALLED AN ANARCHOUS SITUATION. FOR SOME REASON WHEN PEOPLE HAVE COMPLETE FREEDOM TO BE GOOD OR BAD THEY WILL DO SOMETHING BAD. OR LOOK AT IT AS A CHOICE BETWEEN NOBLE OR EVIL. POSITIVE OR NEGATIVE. I WOULD PREFER THAT PERFORMER PARTICIPANTS IN A HAPPENING OPERATE WITH A SENSE OF DISCIPLINE, PROPORTION AND RESPONSIBILITY.

SO THE HAPPENING FOCUSES PEOPLE ONTO THE POSSIBILITIES OF AN OPPORTUNITY TO SEE THEATER IN LIFE, OR LIFE EXPERIENCE AS THEATER.

FOR SEVERAL YEARS I DID FREE FORM HAPPENINGS. NO REHEARSALS. PERFORMER PARTICIPANTS WOULD HAVE NO IDEA WHO EACH OTHER WERE OR WHAT THEY WERE GOING TO DO OR WHAT WOULD TAKE PLACE. I WOULD DESIGN THE PIECE FOR THE SPACE IT WAS GOING

TO HAPPEN IN, USUALLY A LARGE LOFT STUDIO-AREA, SOMETIMES A ROOF, A YARD, A CELLAR, A THEATRE OR, A SEVERAL FLOORS HIGH, RESIDENCE BUILDING.

I WOULD HAVE DIFFERENT AREAS PREPARED. LETS SAY: ① A TABLE ON WHICH SOME CHILDREN'S TOYS, CHOSEN FOR THE SOUNDS THEY MAKE, WERE PLACED.

② A TALL STEPLADDER AND A SHORT STEPLADDER. THESE WOULD BE SO THAT THINGS COULD HAPPEN UP IN THE SPACE

③ A PLATFORM ONE OR TWO FEET HIGH

④ A PHONOGRAPH WITH DIVERSE LPS.
AFRICAN TRIBAL MUSIC
MILITARY MARCHING BANDS
OPERA: CALLAS
ELVIS PRESLEY
A 30'S SWING BAND
NEW ORLEANS MARCHING BAND JAZZ
PERRY COMO 50'S POPSONGS
BILLIE HOLLIDAY, NINA SIMONE
CHINESE MUSIC

⑤ A SOUND CASSETTE PLAYER AND SIMILARLY DIVERSE SOUND CASSETTES

⑥ HAMMER, NAILS, ROPE (CLOTHESLINE) PLASTIC SHEETS OUTDOORS: SPRAY CANS FOR COLOR INDOORS PAINT AND BRUSHES OR SPRAY PAINT USED MINIMALLY

(7) OBJECTS: AN OAR, PIECES OF WOOD, CARDBOARD
BOXES, DIVERSE HATS, MASKS, KITSCH OBJECTS

(8.) ONE OR TWO SLIDE PROJECTORS

(A.) LETS SAY ONE PERSON I HAVE INVITED TO PARTICIPATE
IS ASKED TO GET 50 OR 60 DIAS-FOTO SLIDES. I
WOULD THEN SUGGEST THAT FOR THE FIRST TEN
MINUTES THEY STAND BY THE PROJECTOR AND FROM
TIME TO TIME GO STAND IN ANOTHER PART OF THE
SPACE AND JUST WATCH WHAT IS TAKING PLACE
SHE ASKS ME WHAT WILL BE TAKING PLACE. I ANSWER
THAT I HAVE NO IDEA. BUT ROUGHLY SPEAKING AFTER
TEN MINUTES SHE SHOULD STAND BY THE PROJECTOR,
TURN IT ON AND SHOW SOME DIAS. THEY COME ON OUT
OF FOCUS AND SHE VERY SLOWLY BRINGS THEM INTO
FOCUS. I AND THE OTHERS HAVE AS LITTLE IDEA
AS THE AUDIENCE WHAT THEY WILL BE FOTOS
OF.

(B.) I HAVE INVITED AN ACTOR TO JOIN IN. I GIVE
HIM A COPY OF KRAFT EBING AND ASK HIM TO
FROM TIME TO TIME OPEN IT TO ANY PAGE AND
CHOOSE A SHORT PARAGRAPH AND READ IT ALOUD.
IF HE OPENS THE BOOK TO FULL PAGES OF TEXT,
TO THEN READ ANYWHERE ON THE PAGE TO READ

5 OR 6 SENTENCES. THE NEXT TIME HE FEELS LIKE
READING; TO READ JUST ONE SENTENCE SLOWLY
THE THIRD TIME TO READ A PARAGRAPH OR 10
SENTENCES. THE FOURTH AND PROBABLY LAST
TIME TO READ JUST 3 OR 4 SENTENCES

(C) ONE OR TWO PEOPLE ARE TO HAMMER A NAIL
IN ONE WALL TIE THE STRING TO IT THEN PUT A
NAIL IN ANOTHER WALL, STRETCH AND FASTEN
THE STRING. THEN HANG THE CLEAR PLASTIC
SHEETS TO THE STRING WITH TESA TAPE. IF THE
STRING IS LONG IT WILL SAG IN THE MIDDLE SO
WITH THE TALL STEP LADDER THEY CAN SUPPORT
IT WITH STRINGS TO THE CEILING PERHAPS TO
CEILING LAMPS, ETC. OR OUT DOORS TO OVERHEAD
BRANCHES OF A TREE. THEY CAN PAINT WHATEVER
THEY WANT TO ON IT. I WOULD PREFER THEY WORK
SLOWLY.

(D) A DANCER HAS VOLUNTEERED TO BE IN THE PIECE.
I TELL HER OR HIM IT WILL BE ABOUT 25 TO 30
MINUTES LONG. I SUGGEST THAT AFTER ABOUT THE
FIRST 5 MINUTES THEY DO A WARM UP, LOOSENING UP
EXERCISE ANY WHERE THEN GO TO ANOTHER POINT
AND WATCH FOR A TIME THEN MOVE ABOUT ALWAYS
STOPPING AT SOME POINT AND GOING TO ANOTHER

PLACE TO WATCH. IN ORDINARY THEATER, DANCE, MUSIC YOU ARE ON THE STAGE AND YOU PERFORM. IN A HAPPENING, PARTICULARLY BY ME, YOU CAN GO BEHIND THE AUDIENCE AND SEE HOW IT LOOKS! I WOULD ALSO SUGGEST THAT THE DANCER NOT ALWAYS DANCE BUT SOMETIMES TO MOVE ABOUT WITH NORMAL MOVEMENTS AND SEVERAL TIMES TO FREEZE. IF TWO DANCERS WERE PLANNING TO SAMBA OR FOX TROT I WOULD SUGGEST THAT FROM TIME TO TIME THEY FREEZE AND NOW AND THEN WALK ABOUT OR MOVE SEPERATELY. PERHAPS THEY COULD EXCHANGE COATS, OR SHIRTS OR T-SHIRTS

(E) I WANT TO HAVE A PERSON RIDE THROUGH AND AROUND ON A BICYCLE WITH A PORTABLE RADIO ON ANY STATION. AT LEAST TWICE, NO MORE THAN THREE TIMES. PERHAPS SEVERAL RADIOS

(F) IF THERE WAS A STAIR WELL OR A BALCONY AT SOME POINT I WOULD WANT SOMEONE TO VERY SLOWLY COME DOWN A THICK ROPE. PERHAPS THAT WOULD BE EASIER WITH KNOTS IN IT.

(G) ON THE TABLE WITH THE TOYS THERE ARE CARS THAT MAKE A SIREN OR RATCHETY SOUND, TOY GUNS, SQUEAKY SQUEEZE TOYS, RATTLES, ETC. ONE OR TWO

VOLUNTEERS COULD DO THAT. JUST EXPLORE MAKING SOUNDS BUT FROM TIME TO TIME THEY SHOULD BE STILL AND JUST SOBERLY LISTEN AND WATCH.

(H) I WILL PLAY THE LP'S A CUT OR A SECTION OF THIS ONE AND THAT ONE. RANDOMLY CHOSEN. SOME OF THEM I WILL NOT USE AT ALL. SOMETIMES I WILL PLAY A CONTRASTING LP AND SOUND CASSETTE SIMULT- ANEOUSLY.

THE AUDIENCE IS COMING IN, SOMEONE ASKS ME WHERE WOULD BE THE BEST PLACE TO SIT. NOT HAVING MORE THAN A VAGUE IDEA WHAT WILL HAPPEN, WHEN OR WHERE I WOULD SAY THEY COULD CHANGE THEIR SEAT WHENEVER THEY WANT TO.

I LIKE THE PIECE TO BE SORT OF GOING ON WHEN THE AUDIENCE BEGINS TO COME IN. BITS OF MUSIC ARE PLAYING, THE LIGHTING CHANGES.

THE MOST IMPORTANT THING TO ME IS THAT SILENCE IS AS IMPORTANT AS SOUND AND NOT DOING ANYTHING IS AS EFFECTIVE AS DOING SOMETHING. MOVEMENT AND NON-MOVEMENT, SILENCE AND SOUND. ALL THE MATCHUPS ARE ACCIDENTAL, I AND THE PERFORMERS AND THE AUDIENCE ARE SEEING IT FOR THE FIRST TIME. SO, IT BEGINS OR OPENS LIKE AN UMBRELLA, OR PEELING THE

SKINS FROM AN ONION.

WE ARE ALL OPERATING WITH FAITH TO DO THESE THINGS AND SEE WHAT HAPPENS. I PREPARE A VERY SKETCHY SKELETON AND INVITE PEOPLE TO HANG MEAT ON IT, CONNECT IT UP IN A RANDOM FREEFORM CHANCE OPERATION.

WHAT CAN GO WRONG? LOTS! I AM OFTEN LIKE AN OARSMAN STEERING A RUBBER BOAT THROUGH WHITE-WATER RAPIDS. HA!

A HAPPENING THE WAY I DID THEM FREE-FORM WITH-OUT REHEARSALS IS A LOT LIKE CHINESE WOK COOKING. HOURS OF CHOPPING VEGETABLES AND WHEN THE WOK IS HOT YOU PUT EVERYTHING IN WHILE STIRRING AND IT IS ALL COOKED IN TWO TO THREE MINUTES.

I ALWAYS THINK STRATEGICALLY IN TERMS OF WHAT COULD GO WRONG. ELECTRIC CORDS FROM PROJECTORS, PHONOGRAPHS AND LIGHTS SHOULD BE TAPED TO THE FLOOR SO NOONE WILL ACCIDENTALY KICK IT LOOSE WHILE MOVING ABOUT IN THE DARK PARTS OF THE PIECE. ALSO A PROJECTOR IS AS GOOD AS THE BULB IN IT SO IT SHOULD HAVE A SPARE NEW BULB. ALSO I HAVE A LOT OF DIAS SLIDES SO IF SHE DOESNT SHOW UP FOR SOME REASON I WOULD HAVE SOMEONE FROM THE AUDIENCE DO IT.

I LET THE PIECE TELL ME HOW IT WANTS TO BE. I JUST ENNABLE THE HAPPENING TO HAPPEN.

IF, FOR EXAMPLE I HAD WANTED A CELLIST TO BE IN IT AND AT THE LAST MINUTE SHE CALLED TO SAY, SHE WAS

SORRY BUT SHE WAS STUCK IN PHILADELPHIA AND COULDN'T GET
TO NEW YORK, I WOULDN'T GO CRAZY LOOKING FOR A "LAST MINUTE
CELLIST" I WOULD ASSUME THE PIECE "DIDN'T WANT A CELLO"
AND ACCEPT THAT.

JOHN CAGE ONCE TOLD ME FIGHTING AGAINST LIMITATIONS
IS A WASTE OF TIME AND ENERGY. TO ACCEPT THE LIMITATIONS
AND WORK WITHIN THEM DESTROYS THE LIMITATIONS AND ON
TOP OF THAT YOU ARE WORKING! THEN HE WOULD LAUGH HIS
CRAZY LAUGH.

NOW BACK TO WHAT CAN GO WRONG. THE ACTOR.
I EXPLAIN NOT ONLY WHAT TO DO BUT ALSO WHY. THE
REASON HE SHOULD READ LITTLE PIECES OF TEXT FROM
TIME TO TIME IS SO THAT THE ACTION IS LIKE THERE
ARE SEVERAL BALLS BOUNCING AROUND IN AND OUT
OF THE LIGHT. ANYTHING CONTINUOUS TENDS TO DOMINATE
AND PEOPLE ARE TRAINED BY THEATRE, FILM, AND THE
NOVEL TO LOOK FOR A NARRATIVE CONTINUITY. NON-
MOVEMENT AND NON ACTIVITY IN EQUAL PROPORTION
TO MOVEMENT AND ACTIONS. SILENCE AS IMPORTANT
AS SOUND. DARKNESS AND LIGHT IN VARIETY AND
EVERYTHING NOT JUST ON THE FLOOR BUT UP IN THE
SPACE IN THE ROOM AND THINGS COMING FROM UP
DOWN INTO IT. AND THINGS COMING INTO THE SPACE
AND GOING OUT OF IT. LIKE MORTON FELDMAN'S MUSIC.

SO THE ACTOR BEGINS TO READ. SOUNDS COME
FROM THE TABLE OF TOYS, THE ROPE IS BEING PUT
UP WALL TO WALL, SOMEONE CHANGES THE AFRICAN

TRIBAL MUSIC LP FOR A CUT OF MARCHING BAND
MUSIC. THE ACTOR HAS BEGUN TO READ A FEW LINES.
FROM KRAFT EBING. I CHANGE THE LIGHT SITUATION
AND A SLIDE HAS JAMMED IN THE PROJECTOR. IT TAKES
A MINUTE OR TWO TO FIX AND THE ACTOR IS STILL
READING! HE'S TURNING THE PAGE. I START TO GO
TO HIM BUT ONE OF THE DANCERS HAS PULLED
HER SWEATER UP OVER HER HEAD AND SHE IS INSIDE
THE STEP LADDER AND LIFTING IT, TILTING IT THIS
WAY AND THAT. IN A FEW SECONDS THE BICYCLIST
MIGHT DRIVE THROUGH UNAWARE THAT SOMEONE IS
HOLDING A STEPLADDER HORIZONTALLY! THE ACTOR
TURNS A PAGE AND CONTINUES TO READ. IS HE AN
ACTOR WHO IS SEIZING THE MOMENT TO STEAL THE
SHOW OR IS HE A COMPLETE MORON? A LITTLE OF EACH
I AM AFRAID. SO I GO TO HIM AS HE BEGINS THE 3RD
OR 4TH PAGE OF TEXT. I TAKE HIS ELBOW AND MURMER
IN HIS EAR, "THAT WAS WONDERFUL, COME WITH ME."
SO WE STROLL ARM IN ARM THROUGH THE PERFOR-
MANCE SPACE AND AROUND A CORNER BEHIND
WHICH I HAVE A LOT OF PLUGS AND SOCKETS. I
EXPLAIN TO HIM THAT LIGHTS GO ON AND OFF
BY PUTTING IN OR TAKING OUT PLUGS AND FOR

AWHILE I WOULD LIKE HIM TO LOOK AT THE PIECE AND TURN LIGHTS ON AND OFF RANDOMLY. HE WILL FIND, PERHAPS THAT HE IS ALSO TURNING OFF THE DIA PROJECTOR AND THE PHONOGRAPH AS WELL. IN AN AREA OR COUNTRY WHERE POWER BLACKOUTS ARE COMMON I WOULD USE BATTERY POWERED EQUIPMENT. ALSO, LETS NOT FORGET CANDLES.

SO, YASMIN THIS IS A DESCRIPTION OF A HAPPENING. AN IMPORTANT THING MANY HAPPENING PEOPLE FORGOT WAS HOW TO END IT. SOMETIMES THE AUDIENCES IN THE SIXTIES WOULD SIT FOR 4 OR 5 MINUTES WAITING FOR THE NEXT THING TO HAPPEN ONLY TO SLOWLY REALIZE IT WAS OVER.

BEING IN A HAPPENING IS TO TAKE PART IN SPONTANEOUS CREATION, CONSTANT OPPORTUNITY TO MAKE CHOICES. TO BECOME THE COLLEAGUE OF THE COMPOSER, HAPPENING MAKER. A HAPPENING IS ABOUT THE NATURE AND FUNCTION OF ARTS. THE RELATIONSHIP AND MIRRORING ONE ARTS TO EACH OTHER. THEIR OVERLAPS, INTERPENETRATIONS, SIMILARITIES AND INTERMEDIA AREAS. IN TIME AND SPACE. THE PROCESS IS THE DIRECTOR. EVERYONE IS WRITING AND DIRECTING THEIR OWN PART SPONTANEOUSLY. DECIDING/CHOOSING WHAT TO DO NEXT.

Al Hansen, Hershey Bar Kite, 1973, Hershey bar wrappers on board, 47 x 57". Collection Bibbe Hansen.

Al Hansen, Kipling East West Venus Box, 1991, mixed media in wooden box, 12 x 10". Collection Bibbe Hansen.

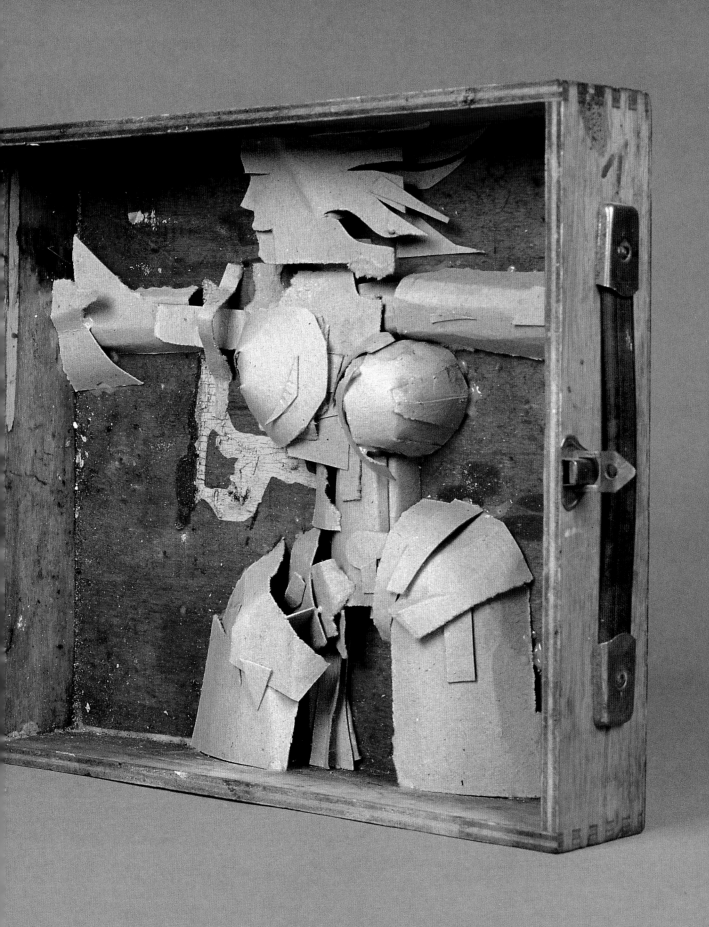

neighbors and even enemies.
Despite all, the tone of this
little import is plucky and
cheerful, like a family theatri-

place. The audience loved it.
You don't have to be Jewish
to love Dzigan's show, but you
do have to be Yiddish.

"LOTS OF LAUGHS AND THE SEX
PLAY IS IN THE OPEN. A VERY
HIGH CLASS EXAMPLE OF THE
GENRE. TAKING OFF WHERE
LEERY COP-OUTS LIKE 'BOB &
CAROL & TED & ALICE' ARE
GROUNDED. IN THIS ONE YOU
GET, AN ORGY THAT'S AN ORGY!"
—Judith Crist, New York Magazine

All the
Loving
Couples

RELEASED BY U-M FILM DISTRIBUTORS INC.
COLOR BY MOVIELAB

NEW EMBASSY 46th St.
Broadway at 46 St.: PL 7-2465
10, 12, 1:30, 3, 4:45, 6:15, 8, 9:45, 11:30 , 1 AM

New LOEW'S
Orpheum
1, 2:30, 4, 5:30, 7, 8:30, 10, 11:30

DUE TO OVERWHELMING RESPONSE TO SEE "ALL THE LOVING COUPLES"
THE NEW EMBASSY WILL BE OPEN ALL NIGHT.

OH! WH
LOVELY

The Paris

NEW, AMAZING
3-D
IN LIVING COLOR
2 FIRST RUN HITS

FUNNY HILLS

851

Quinn, lover of the art of make-believe.

?

« L'idea di dotare il nostro centro di apparecchi televisivi mi venne quando seppi che Bobby, uno scimpanzé di proprietà di una famiglia di Santa Barbara, adorava guardare i film western. Pensai di fare un esperimento qui al Centro e, attraverso un appello, in breve tempo ci ospitiamo, la TV è un passatempo meraviglioso: si annoiano, poverine, e non hanno la possibilità le libera dalla noia, dalle nevrosi, dagli scatti d'ira. I loro gusti sono ben precisi: amano tutt

Al Hansen 1974.

RAY JOHNSON
44 WEST 7 STREET
LOCUST VALLEY
NEW YORK 11560

August 27, 1973

Dear Gypsy Rose Lee,

RAY JOHNSON
44 WEST 7 STREET
LOCUST VALLEY
NEW YORK 11560

Mr. Al Hansen
40 Prince Street
NYCity, NY 10012

PHILIP MORRIS

Mr. L.Hansen
Rolandstraße 92

5000 Köln 1

Nov. 22, 1990

Dear Mr. Hansen,

gladly I can let you know that we will put 3000 Marlboro Cigarettes at
your disposal to support your artistic work.

We would appreciate receiving a photo of your finished work of art.

Please let us know if it is possible for you to mention the support of
Marlboro in a positive way in your PR context.

Please let us know the exact adress where the cigarettes should be
delivered to.

I tried to call you - but it appears that your phone is out of order.

Best wishes and kind regards,

PHILIP MORRIS GMBH

i.A. Nicole Remlinger

Vorsitzender des Aufsichtsrates:
Walter Thoma
Vorsitzender der Geschäftsführung:
Paul Hendrys

Geschäftsführer:
Dr. Dietrich Flugs
Hans Fluri
Knut Föckler
Lauro Peuckert

Sitz der Gesellschaft:
München
Registergericht München
HRB 49432

PHILIP MORRIS GmbH
Postfach 70 14 29
Fallstraße 40
8000 München 70
Telefon: 089/72 47-0
Telex: 5 23 957 mpol d
Telefax: 089/72 47-12 27

SOUND. WIND IN THE EAVES, A DRIPPING FAUCET. BED
SPRING SQUEEK. OUR MOTHERS HEART BEAT. THE ROAR OF
A FOOTBALL CROWD. TRAFFIC: TOOT TOOT, HONK, HONK!
THE TICKING OF A CLOCK. NUNS SPEAK IN WHISPERS.

M.F.: I DON'T EVEN KNOW WHAT IT WAS TO BE A COMPOSER.
JC: WELL YOU SAID EARLIER — AND I'M AGREEING WITH YOU, AND
I REMEMBER DOING IT — IT WAS BEING DEEP IN THOUGHT (BOTH
LAUGH).
M.F.: YES, THAT'S ALL I'M LEFT WITH! I FEEL THAT THIS THOUGHT WAS
TAKEN ~~FROM ME~~ AWAY FROM ME. THAT'S IT.
JC: NO, BUT THERE'S ANOTHER WAY TO BE A COMPOSER, SURELY.
THERE COULD AT LEAST BE THIS ONE WE'VE ALREADY MENTIONED
— SOMEONE DEEP IN THOUGHT WHO'S CONSTANTLY INTERRUPTED.
MF: LIKE BACH!
JC: OR THERE COULD BE, WHAT I'VE SUGGESTED, I THINK, IN SOME OF MY
WORK, SOMEONE WHO DOESN'T HAVE ANY THOUGHTS AND SO CAN'T BE
SAID TO BE EITHER SHALLOW OR DEEP AND WHO SIMPLY SETS SOMETHING
GOING, THAT EITHER HAS SOUNDS IN IT OR DOESN'T HAVE SOUNDS IN IT,
THAT ENABLES NOT ONLY OTHER PEOPLE, BUT HIMSELF, TOO, TO EXPERIENCE.
I GUESS, IN MY CASE, THAT IT GOES OUT OF THOUGHT INTO EXPERIENCE. THIS WAS
CERTAINLY ONE OF THE THINGS THAT SHOWED UP, WHEN THE FRENCHMEN,
HEADED BY BOULEZ, BEGAN TO OBJECT TO MY WORK AND IDEAS: THEY
OBJECTED TO THE NOTION THAT MUSIC WAS MADE OF SOUND.
MF: YES, I ALWAYS THOUGHT IT WAS EXTRAORDINARY. IT WAS LIKE THE
MEDICAL PROFESSION OBJECTING TO THE FACT THAT SEMMELWEIS ←
SAID THEY SHOULD WASH THEIR HANDS BEFORE THEY PERFORM AN
OPERATION (BOTH LAUGH). (IN 1847 HUNGARY)
JC: NO, I THINK ONE OF THE THINGS THAT HAS HAPPENED IS THAT IT'S
BECOME CLEAR THAT WE CAN BE, NOT JUST WITH OUR MINDS, BUT WITH OUR
WHOLE BEING, RESPONSIVE TO SOUND. AND THAT THAT SOUND DOESN'T
HAVE TO BE THE COMMUNICATION OF SOME DEEP THOUGHT. THEY CAN BE

JUST A SOUND. NOW THAT SOUND COULD GO IN ONE EAR AND OUT THE OTHER, OR IT COULD GO IN ONE EAR, PERMEATE THE BEING, TRANSFORM THE BEING, AND THEN PERHAPS GO OUT, LETTING THE NEXT ONE IN (BOTH LAUGH) AND THEN, WHETHER OR NOT AN IDEA DEVELOPED... YOU KNOW, THE HARDEST THING IN THE WORLD, OF COURSE, IS TO HAVE A HEAD WITHOUT ANY IDEAS IN IT.

PAGES 25 AND 27 OF MORTON FELDMAN/JOHN CAGE, RADIO HAPPENINGS, CONVERSATIONS-GESPRÄCHE. PUB MUSIK TEXTE, COLOGNE, GERMANY

IN JOHN CAGES CLASS WE BEGAN TO DISCUSS THE QUALITY OF ANNOYING SOUNDS PARTICULARLY FINGERNAILS ON A BLACKBOARD AND THE SOUND OF A KNIFE CUTTING CARDBOARD... JOHN SUGGESTED ONE COULD REPEAT THIS SOUND ENDLESSLY AND ONE MIGHT BECOME ACCLIMATED TO THE SOUND, OR ITS AFFECT WOULD GET WORN OUT. FROM WORKING IN COLLAGE THE SOUND OF A KNIFE CUTTING CARDBOARD DOESN'T BOTHER ME. I DON'T THINK I COULD STAND THE FIRST FIFTY OR HUNDRED FINGERNAIL SCRAPING SOUNDS ON A BLACKBOARD. I HAVE NO INTEREST IN HEARING IT ONCE.

ONCE, SIGMA POLKE HAD A CONFLICT OF EVENTS SO I TOOK OVER FOR HIM AS SUMMER ART GUEST PROFESSOR AT THE ART SCHOOL IN HAMBURG. HAMBURG IS A WONDERFUL CITY BUT PART OF MY EXPERIENCE THERE WAS AWFUL. GERMAN ART SCHOOLS AND AKADEMIES ARE RUN IN AN UNUSUAL WAY. TO JUSTIFY THE EXPENSE TO THE TOWN OR STATE COUNCIL MANY OF THE TEACHERS ARE CHOSEN BECAUSE THEY HAVE A NAME. THAT MEANS THAT WELL MORE THAN HALF THE ART PROFESSORS IN GERMAN ART SCHOOLS ARE NOT TRAINED TO TEACH OR HAVE THE VAGUEST IDEA HOW THIS IS DONE. HAVING STUDIED FOR A BACHELOR OF SCIENCE, IN ART EDUCATION DEGREE AT PRATT INSTITUTE IN BROOKLYN I AM ALWAYS ASTONISHED IN MY TRAVELS TO REGULARLY MEET ARTISTS EARNING MONEY AS TEACHERS WHO HAVE NOT THE VAGUEST IDEA WHAT TEACHING IS OR HOW IT WORKS. BUT ART IS MAGIC AND THE ART EXPERIENCE IS A SPECIAL ONE SO, HALF THE TIME IT DOESN'T MATTER. BECAUSE THEY ARE, LETS SAY FOR LACK OF A BETTER

WORD, "FAMOUS", IT IS UNDERSTOOD THAT THEY OFTEN HAVE COMMITMENTS ELSEWHERE. THE SCHOOL OFFICIALS LOOK THE OTHER WAY AND THE ARTIST SHOWS UP INFREQUENTLY. TWO DAYS A MONTH WOULD BE A HIGH RATE OF PERFORMANCE FOR MANY OF THEM. THE ART SCHOOLS ARE VERY CROWDED. THERE ARE STUDIOS AND LIVE-IN STUDIOS FOR THE ART PROFESSORS. THE ART PROFESSOR HAS AN ASSISTANT, HE TAKES CARE OF BUSINESS WHILE THE PROFESSOR IS AWAY. THERE ARE SOME STUDIOS TOO FOR GUEST PROFESSORS. THE ART SCHOOL IS USUALLY A SMALL EMPIRE. THERE ARE FRIENDS OF THE EMPIRE. FRIENDS OF THE EMPIRE HAVE UNLIMITED ACCESS TO THESE STUDIOS. AT HAMBURG ALL THE STUDIOS WERE FULL. SOMEONE WAS LIVING AND WORKING IN EACH OF THE PROFESSORS STUDIOS AND FRIENDS OF THE EMPIRE WERE OCCUPYING ALL THE GUEST PROFESSOR STUDIOS, HOWEVER MANY THERE ARE, SO, I WAS BILLETED TO A SMALL OFFICE STORE-ROOM IN THE ARCHITECTURE BUILDING. IT HAD A SORT OF HOSPITAL OR ARMY BED AND A TABLE. AND TWO CHAIRS. IN THE NEXT ROOM WAS THE HEIZUNG OR STROM ZAHLER AND IT TICKED LOUDLY AT NIGHT. TICK, TICK, TICK, TICK, TICK, TICK, TICK, TICK. THIS CAN MAKE YOU NUTS. IT WASN'T LOUD DURING THE DAY BUT AT NIGHT IT WAS QUITE LOUD. AND ANNOYING. I REMEMBERED WHAT JOHN CAGE HAD SAID YEARS BEFORE. I WOULD COUNT THE TICKS IT WOULD TAKE 5 OR 6,000 BEFORE I COULD DROP OFF TO SLEEP. IT WAS RIGHT ON THE STREET SO IF TRAFFIC NOISE WOKE ME UP THERE WOULD BE THE TICK, TICK, TICK, TICK, TICK SOUND. I GOT EXTRA PILLOWS AND WRAPPED A TOWEL AROUND MY HEAD BUT YOU COULD STILL HEAR THE SOUND. tick, tick, tick, tick, IT WAS SUMMER AND A LOT OF THE REGULAR STUDENTS WERE AWAY SO I BEGAN TO CRASH AROUND IN ROOMS OF THE DIFFERENT COOP FLATS AROUND THE SCHOOL. IN THIS WAY I WAS INVOLVED WITH A LOT OF THE STUDENTS IN AN EXTRA INSTITUTIONAL WAY AND THIS PART OF THE FEW MONTHS AS A GUEST ART PROFESSOR WAS VERY ENJOYABLE AND INTERESTING.

I WAS BORN DURING THE YEAR OF THE FIRST SOUND MOVIE. AL JOLSON IN THE JAZZ SINGER. 1927.

BEING ABLE TO RECORD SOUND ON TAPE CAME OUT OF WORLD WAR II. THE FIRST RECORDERS USED WIRE. IN THE LATE FORTIES IN NEW ORLEANS, LOUISIANA, I PLANNED WITH RANDOLPH BAY TO MAKE A WIRE RECORDING OF SOUNDS IN THE CITY PARTICULARLY PILE DRIVERS HAMMERING LARGE COLUMNS INTO THE EARTH, THE PNEUMATIC SOUND OF BUS AND TRAM DOORS OPENING AND CLOSING, BIRD SONG, TRAFFIC, THE SOUND OF KNIVES, FORKS, AND SPOONS IN A RESTAURANT, THE SOUND OF WOMEN'S HEELS ON PAVE-MENT. IT WAS TO END WITH THE SOUND OF DROPS OF WATER COMING FROM A FAUCET. I FELT THAT WOULD SYMBOLIZE ETERNITY. I NEVER MADE THIS SOUND POEM BUT IF I DID IT TODAY I WOULD USE THE SAME SOUND IDEAS AS THEY STILL FASCINATE ME.

THEY USED TO SAY OF THRIFTY BUSINESSMEN THAT THEY USED EVERY PART OF THE PIG BUT ITS SQUEAL. DITER ROTH HAD DONE SOUND TAPES USING DOGS BARKING AND I THOUGHT IT WOULD BE INTERESTING TO RECORD PIGS SQUEALING BUT I NEVER DID IT. MY ONLY ACCESS TO PIGS WAS THE SLAUGHTERHOUSE IN THE WEST FORTIES OF MANHATTAN WHEN I WAS THE ASSISTANT ART EDITOR OF CHEMICAL ENGINEERING MAGAZINE AT McGRAW-HILL PUBLISHING COMPANY WHEN IT WAS IN THE GREEN BUILDING ON WEST 42 ST. OFF TIMES SQUARE. THAT WAS IN THE MIDDLE FIFTIES AND JUST A FEW YEARS

—4—

AGO, IN THE LATE EIGHTIES I CAME UPON A STORY
IN THE INTERNATIONAL HERALD TRIBUNE ABOUT A
COMPOSER WHO TAPED PIG SQUEALS. HE WAS PROB-
ABLY MOTIVATED BY THE SAME SAYING THAT GAVE
ME THE IDEA.

JOHN CAGE ONCE SAID THAT ANY SOUND CAN BE
MUSIC AND MORTON FELDMAN SAID, "YES, BUT NOT
EVERYONE IS AN ARTIST." I THINK ANYONE CAN BE
AN ARTIST. I THINK EVERYONE IS AN ARTIST IT IS
JUST THAT ART DOESN'T WANT OR NEED EVERYONE
TO DO IT. MANY ARE CALLED, FEW ARE CHOSEN.
THERE SEEMS TO ME, FROM MY EXPERIENCE IN THE
ART WORLDS OF AMERICAN CITIES, NORWEGIAN
CITIES, DUTCH CITIES, DANISH, GERMAN AND
ITALIAN CITIES AS WELL AS VIENNA, PARIS,
PRAGUE, AND SWITZERLAND, THAT THERE ARE
ALWAYS ALMOST TOO MANY ARTISTS FOR THE
CULTURE SYSTEM OF A PLACE TO USE OR TAKE
CARE OF.

FROM READING SERGEI EISENSTEIN'S FILM FORM AND
FILM SENSE IT DAWNED ON ME ANY SIGHT COULD GO WITH
ANY SOUND. AT THE TIME I WAS LIVING WITH MY SECOND
WIFE MARVYNE LEVY GLASER IN AN APARTMENT BUILDING
ON WEST 24TH STREET. IT WAS ACROSS THE STREET

FROM A MONSTER RESIDENTIAL BUILDING CALLED LONDON TERRACE. HITCHCOCK COULD HAVE MADE A FILM FROM MY FLAT CALLED FRONT WINDOW. THERE WAS A GREAT DEAL OF ACTIVITY, PEOPLE COMING AND GOING. I LIKED TO LISTEN TO MUSIC WHILE I WORKED AND I WAS FOND OF PUTTING SEVEN OR EIGHT DIVERSE LP'S ON OUR RECORD PLAYER. SO IT WOULD BE STAN KENTON, FRENCH MILITARY BAND MARCHES, FRED ASTAIRE, BILLY HOLIDAY, ESKIMO DOG DRUM SONGS, EDITH PIAF, THE DORSEY BROTHERS ETC.. WHILE WORKING I WOULD FROM TIME TO TIME STAND UP AND STRETCH AND LOOK OUT THE WINDOW. I SUDDENLY REALIZED THAT EACH TIME I DID THAT, WHAT I WAS SEEING WORKED PERFECTLY WITH WHAT I WAS HEARING. PEOPLE WALKING DOGS, WAITING IN CARS FOR GIRLS TO COME DOWN FROM UPSTAIRS, A WOMAN COMBING AND BRUSHING HER HAIR THROUGH ONE WINDOW, ANOTHER GIRL ENDLESSLY TRYING ON CLOTHES IN DIFFERENT ENDLESS COMBINATIONS. A WORKING GIRL SEEING WHAT GOES WITH WHAT. I REALIZED WE ARE TRAINED BY WATCHING FILMS AND TV ALL OUR LIFE TO ACCEPT THE SOUND TRACK. ALMOST ANY SOUND TRACK.

ONCE, I WAS SITTING WITH CHRIS NEWMAN, THE COMPOSER, PAINTER, POET, AND SOME OTHERS, TALKING AND DRINKING.

FOR A BIT WE WERE DISCUSSING COMPOSERS AND SOME-
ONE ASKED CHRIS WHAT HE THOUGHT OF MOZART. CHRIS
SAID HE LIKED MOZART BUT HE HAD A PROBLEM THERE
AS MOZART'S MUSIC TODAY IS NEVER HEARD ON THE
HARPSICHORDS IT WAS WRITTEN FOR. THE MODERN
GRAND PIANO DIDN'T EXIST IN MOZART'S TIME.

I HAVE A SIMILAIR PROBLEM WITH TECHNO MUSIC
AS ITS SUPPOSED TO BE HEARD WHILE DOING ECSTASY
SPEED. ONE'S SPEEDED UP HEART BEAT AND BREATHING
WORKS WITH THE SOUND TO MAKE A TRIP. I HAVE
LISTENED TO TECHNO FOR HOURS ON BRITISH FORCES
RADIO AND AT THE END OF A HALF HOUR OF TECHNO
THE DISK JOCKEY WOULD TELL THE TITLES AND THE
GROUPS AND THERE IS NO DIVISION BETWEEN THE
DIFFERENT GROUPS SOUND BEATS THAT I CAN DISCERN.
I HAVE ALWAYS BEEN A CHAMPION OF THE NEW BUT
TECHNO REALLY LEAVES ME BEHIND. LIKE JOHN
CAGE I FEEL DEEPLY THAT SILENCE AND SOUND
ARE EQUALLY IMPORTANT. I ALSO DEEPLY PREFER
NON MOVEMENT, OR BEING STILL, AS BEING AS
IMPORTANT AS MOVEMENT IN A DANCE PIECE.

THE SOUND OF SILENCE. RAIN ON THE ROOF.
A FAROFF TRAIN.

Al Hansen

I WAS WALKING WITH JOHN LENNON AND YOKO ONCE AND I WAS WHISTLING AND TRYING TO REMEMBER THE CLARINET RIDE IN AN OLD NEW ORLEANS DIXIELAND JAZZ TUNE. I THINK IT WAS PART OF RAMPART STREET PARADE, BOB CROSBY + THE BOBCATS (BING'S BROTHER), AT THIS WRITING I HAVE THE CLARINET THING CONFUSED WITH CLARINET MARMALADE ANOTHER DIXIELAND TUNE. ANYWAY LENNON WAS TALKING TO YOKO AND HE TURNED TO ME AND SAID, "THATS REALLY OLD, MAN." "YEAH," I SAID. "NEW ORLEANS." "THAT'S ITALIAN," HE NAMED A COMPOSER FROM THE FIFTEEN OR SIXTEEN HUNDREDS, I WHISTLED IT AGAIN. "ITS HIM." JOHN SAID. "NAH, C'MON ITS DIXIELAND." THEN HE WENT ON ABOUT THE COMPOSER WHO WAS OBSCURE AND LITTLE KNOWN. I SAID IT WAS POSSIBLE THAT THE COMPOSER'S WORK HAD BEEN PERFORMED IN LOUISIANA AND SLAVES HEARD IT.

THIS WAS BROUGHT TO MIND LISTENING TO A PROGRAM OF ITALIAN FOLK MUSIC ON THE GERMAN CHANNEL IN LYKKE ROSENKRANT'S KITCHEN IN AMAGER. SHE KEEPS IT [HER RADIO] ON POLAND BUT WAVELENGTH THE RADIO WANDERS AS MUCH AS A HERTZ BOUNCE WAVE SO IT HAD WALKED OVER OR DOWN OR UP TO THE GERMAN CHANNEL. IT WAS GENOESE SONG AND IT HAD AS MUCH A SENSE OR FEELING OF WATER IN IT AS HAWAIIAN, POLYNESIAN, OR ESKIMO MUSIC. IT ALSO SUBTLY RECALLED THE BEATLES.

ON LYKKE'S KITCHEN STOVE THERE ARE 4 BURNERS. THE RIGHT FRONT ONE IS FOR BOILING AND WILL BOIL A POT OR KETTLE OF WATER IN 4 OR 5 MINUTES, WHEREAS THE OTHERS TAKE 15 OR 20 OR MORE TO BRING WATER TO A BOIL. THE 'HEAD' MUST HAVE LARGER HOLES AROUND ITS EDGE TO EMIT MORE GAS FOR MORE HEAT. I WAS WONDERING IF ONE COULD DRILL THE HOLES LARGER IN ANOTHER BURNERS GAS HEAD AND HAVE A QUICKER FIRE.

THE FAMOUS <u>DENNIS HOPPER</u> INTERVIEW

I think Apex Magazine is trying to become trendy. They want me to do a piece on Dennis Hopper. What the hell does Dennis Hopper – who is a genius – have to do with art in the Cologne area in particular and with Germany and Europe in general? I am still trying to get a Guest Professorship in a German art school. Most Fluxus people, while very foxy, do not know much about art. In fact many Fluxus people do not know much about anything except getting ignition on bar tabs (dekkels), not sharing information and stabbing each other in the back – usually gratuitously. For the fun of it.

Dennis Hopper is, of course, important to any facet of art. He is an interesting, always rewarding actor; he comes off the wall and from the unexpected corner. What happens in the movies and acting is highly relevant to art, drawing paper manufacturing, beer & alcohol consumption at the Paris Bar in Berlin, Cafe Victor in Copenhagen, Chinn's in Cologne, Die Oul in Dusseldorf, triangulated with pastel, aquarelle and linen canvas sales in Tutti Paletti, Perl Paint, etc. divided by One Person Shows, 1/2 of all art sales minus artist's dekkels and palimony internationally. Luxembourg, Sweden and Spain are excluded from this averaging out system because I say so. Being a genius is not all the fun and games many people think but one has automatically the right to refuse certain data.

Then Dexter Gordon died of constellational misuse and bad luck. And Wolfgang keeps yelling I must do an interview with Dennis Hopper for the Basel Kunst Messe Apex Magazine. For several days I tried to call Screen Actor's Guild and ask for management. This is how you get your claws into a famous actor for an interview. I asked Apex to rent me VHS cassettes of seven Dennis Hopper movies. At my secret villa studio in Maastricht, Holland (I can't seem to land a teaching job there either) I have all the equipment to look at four Dennis Hopper films at once. Dexter Gordon dying is enough to tear Copenhagen apart and they want me to drop everything and do an interview with Dennis Hopper!

They have decided to open the Venice Biennale a month earlier this year. End of May I am supposed to be houseguesting with Neapolitan friends who want to present me to their nubile fifteen year old black mistresses in Melindi, Kenya on the Indian Ocean. But I have to be in Venice! I want to write about how much I would like to be an art professor so I can stop running in and out of Germany and settle in a bit. Maybe even learn German a little better finally. But they want me to write about beautiful, stoned, cunning, wonderful Dennis fucking Hopper!

And now the gray eminence has died. Ingo Kummel died at 9:00 this morning while Lisa and Jean Louis Okito Cieslik were driving my oldest grandson Beck Hansen to the Koln Bonn Flughaven. Ingo died. Dexter Gordon died, Bob Watts died, Robert Filliou died,

Andre Thompkins died and Joe Beuys died. My father died - Nicholas A. Hansen 93 1/2 hears old. Helmut Qualtinger died. Everyone I know is dying and they want me to fucking interview Dennis Fucking Hopper...for Apex! What is Apex becoming: Andy's Interview? Vogue Magazine? Wolkankreutzer? A threat to Spex?

They opened up Ingo's head to look for what they thought was a tumor and they found a secret compartment where he has stashed a Beuys, 4 Polkes, 8 Charlie Bananas, a Michael Butee, 3 Al Hansens, an unsigned Dieter Roth and a Meret Oppenheim! Ingo was a very special, unique person. I think an important part of success is to be a little defect. A great work of art to me is one that gives me butterflies in the stomach and hackles on the neck at the same time. Nothing verbal needed. Feeling. You feel it. To me a great work of art is not sure whether it is great or not.

Joseph Beuys, my father, Robert Filliou, Andre Thomkins, Bob Watts, Chet Baker, Dexter Gordon, and not Ingo Kummel. And Wolfgang Apex wants me to do an interview with Dennis Hopper. Dexter used to hold his saxophone out to the audience when they applauded. He was saying, "I didn't do it babies. The saxophone did it."

It is a sweet May night this end of the first day of May in 1990. I write this in Roland Eck at the bottom of Merowinger. The ground has opened up now that it has finally turned warm. And all the trees are budding. The night air makes one pleased with being alive. The body is the package the spirit comes in. Evolpost. At death the body goes down and the spirit, the best, goes up into the sky of our hearts.

Lots will be written about Ingo Kummel that is chronologically factual. I think about his wonderful sons Cain and Thorsten. I didn't know his daughter. I think about wonderful Anne Bahne. We had talked often about a party program for the year 2000 . . . 9 years out. If I make it you will be there Ingo, Dennis Hopper as well. Ingo Kummel died this morning at 9 AM because they couldn't get the paintings out of his head. Dexter Gordon died a few days before at 12:50 Round about morning and Roundabout Midnight.

Al Hansen Roland Eck Bar
Sudstadt 5 Koln 1
1 AM 2 May 1990

NEW REPUBLIC ROBOT SHOES IN THE SWIM
OCEAN ROMANCES THE BINARY REIFICATION
OF SCHIZOPHRENIA COMPUTER DREAMS LADY
PINK THE LAST TRIBE YESTERDAY, TODAY
AND TOMORROW TRANSLUCENT TRANS-
MIGRATION ART CITY PRESENT TENSE 50%
ANOTHER MISUNDERSTANDING ATTITUDE
ART THE ELECTRONIC CHURCH DREAMLAND
BURNS TRICKING THE EYE 88 TANGOS SCOWL
HOLDING BACK TEARS INTERPRETATION OF
SEX AND CAPITAL ECSTASY UNLIMITED L.A.
LUNCHEONETTE DON'T CLIMB MT. EVEREST TO
REACH THE VALLEY OF THE DOLLS TINKERBELL
ALWAYS TAKES A TAXI. RUNNING SCARED THE
GREENING OF A DRINK LIKE A DREAM COME INTO
IMPLEMENTATION THE "YES" MACHINE FREE BEER
BOHEMOS

MAKERS AND LOOKERS

THERE ARE THINGS ONE UNDERSTANDS, KNOWS, FEELS IN ONE'S GUT AND BONES. WAYS ONE OPERATES IN DIVERSE SITUATIONS BUT IT IS ALL UNCONCIOUS, SUB OR UNDER CONSCIOUS. ONE CANNOT ARTICULATE IT OR THEM IN WORDS AND THEN SOMEONE SAYS IT IN A SIMPLE WAY AND IT COMES UP TO THE SURFACE, GETS FUSED INTO THE NOW ACTIVELY. I HAVE HAD THESE EXPERIENCES REGULARLY. I FEEL VERY LUCKY AND PLEASED. I HAD SUCH A SIMPLE ENLIGHTENMENT FROM THE ART AND COMMUNICATIONS PHILOSOPHER ALFRED NORTH WHITEHEAD. HE POSED THE WHITEHEAD SPLIT THAT IS THE DIFFERENCE BETWEEN HOW AN ART WORK IS PERCEIVED BY THE MAKER AS OPPOSED TO HOW IT IS SEEN BY AN OBSERVER. THERE IS NO WAY THE MAKER CAN SEE AN ARTWORK THE WAY THE OBSERVER CAN. IT IS JUST NOT POSSIBLE UNLESS ONE HAD ALZHEIMERS DISEASE. A GOOD THING ABOUT ALZHEIMERS DISEASE IS THAT ONE IS ALWAYS MAKING NEW FRIENDS.

THERE IS NO WAY AN OBSERVER CAN EXPERIENCE A WORK IN THE SAME WAY THE MAKER CAN. PROFESSIONAL CRITICS, MUSEUM AND GALLERY PEOPLE AND COLLECTORS LIKE TO VISIT THE STUDIO WHERE THE WORK IS IN THE WORKSHOP.

COMPARED TO AN ANTISEPTIC GALLERY OR MUSEUM EXHIBITION SPACE ONE IS MUCH CLOSER TO HOW THE WORK WAS MADE. A GALLERY IS PURPOSEFULLY ANTISEPTIC. ABSOLUTELY NOTHING MUST INTRUDE ON THE POTENTIAL BUYERS OBSERVATION OF ART WORKS. IN FACT YOU CAN TELL A PROFESSIONAL GALLERY PERSON BECAUSE THEY WILL NEVER WALK BETWEEN AN ARTWORK AND SOMEONE LOOKING AT IT.

AN INTERESTING THING ABOUT 20th CENTURY ART AND PHILOSOPHIES LIKE EXISTENTIALISM AND ZEN BUDDHISM IS THAT THEY FREED US UP TO THE POINT WHERE WE CAN CONSIDER ANY-THING AS ART. THAT IS TO SAY THAT ANYTHING CAN BE CONSIDERED OR ENTERTAINED AS HAVING AESTHETIC POSSIBILITIES. WITH THE POPULARITY OF ART LOOKERS VISITING AN ART MAKERS SPACE THIS CAUSES SOME FOOLISH BUT INTERESTING CONTRETEMPS. A VISITOR WILL SAY "I LIKE <u>THAT</u> PIECE," AND THE

ARTIST SAYS, "IT ISN'T FINISHED, I HAVE TO PUT A BLUE PAPER IN THE UPPER RIGHT HAND CORNER, THEN I'M GOING TO DRAW A MICKEY MOUSE ON THAT YELLOW AREA CENTER LEFT AND THEN I'M GOING TO GLUE SOME BURNT MATCHES HERE AND THERE..." "NO, NO, NO," THE VISITOR SAYS, "DON'T TOUCH IT, ITS PERFECT THE WAY IT IS!"

I HAVE LEFT BEHIND ME ODDS AND ENDS OF UNFINISHED PIECES, NOW AND THEN A PERSON WILL SEND A PHOTOGRAPH OF AN UNFINISHED WORK AND ASK ME TO SIGN THE PHOTOGRAPH. SOMETIMES THEY BRING IT TO ME AND I TELL THEM THAT I WILL FINISH IT AND SIGN IT FOR A FEE. I HAD A SHOW WITH SPIEGEL GALERIE IN 1974 OF HERSHEY'S BAR WRAPPER COLLAGES. THE WORK WAS TAKEN TO THE GALLERY FROM STEPHAN WEWERKA'S STUDIO IN THE TRAJANSTR. BY ACCIDENT AN UNFINISHED PIECE WAS TAKEN ALONG. IT WAS ABOUT 50 X 60 cm THE HIP AND THIGH, THE ONE HIP AND ONE THIGH OF A VENUS FIGURE WAS

THERE AND I DO FULL FIGURES OF VENUSES AND GODDESSES NOT JUST ONE HIP. AND IT WAS UNSIGNED. DURING THE FLUXUS VIRUS SHOW IN 1992 ONE OF CHRISTEL SCHUPPENHAUER'S GALLERY PEOPLE SHOWED ME A FOTO OF THIS UNFINISHED HARDLY BEGUN PIECE. SHE SAID "WHATS THE DATE?". I SAID," THERE'S NO DATE ITS NOT FINISHED BUT IT WAS BEGUN IN 1973" SHE SAID," WE WOULD LIKE YOU TO SIGN IT." I SAID, " I CAN'T SIGN IT, LOOK AT IT, IT'S UNFINISHED. WHERE DOES THIS COME FROM?" "HEINZ STUNKE." SHE SAID. I SAID," IT'S NOT SIGNED AND THEREFORE NOT PAID FOR. TELL HIM I'LL FINISH IT AND SIGN IT FOR 5,000 DM. A MONTH OR SO LATER CHRISTAL HAD A SMALL COLLAGE, MADE MOSTLY OF R'S, SILVER R'S FROM HERSHEY'S CHOCOLATE BAR PAPERS. THEY WERE DIFFERENT SIZES. READING IT ONE GOT THE SOUND OF THE BUZZ OF PROPELLOR AIRCRAFT. I REMEMBERED IT, IN 1973

I HAD GIVEN IT TO EVA STUNKE, NOW DE-
CEASED. IT WAS TITLED, "THE RED BARON,"
(MANFRED VON RICHTOFEN THE WWI GERMAN
AIR ACE.) THE PRICE WAS DM 30,000. THIS PIECE
IS A LITTLE LESS THAN TWO BEER DECKELS HIGH
AND 3/4 OF A BEER DECKEL WIDE. SO, MY OFFER
TO FINISH THE 50 X 60 cm PIECE FOR DM 5,000
WAS LIKE INVITING ~~OFFERING~~ HERR STUNKE TO LUNCH BY
COMPARISON. I SAW HERR STUNKE AROUND KÖLN
IN PUBLIC INFREQUENTLY. WE ALWAYS SMILED
AND NODDED TO EACH OTHER BUT NEVER SPOKE.
A YEAR LATER, I HAD AN EXHIBITION WITH
GALERIE FRANK BERND IN KÖLN. AFTER
THE SHOW OPENED HE SHOWED ME A PICTURE
OF THIS SAME BEGUN/UNFINISHED PIECE.
"HERR STUNKE HAS THIS PIECE AND WOULD
LIKE YOU TO SIGN IT." "IF IT'S UNSIGNED, IT'S
NOT PAID FOR," I ANSWERED. "WHAT CAN WE DO?"
FRANK ASKED. "TELL HIM I'LL FINISH IT AND
SIGN IT FOR DM 7,000."

THE PERFECT LOVER IS A PHANTOM
FAMOUS MOVIE STARS ARE PHANTOMS
THERE IS A PHANTOM AROUND THE CORNER
BILLIONAIRES ARE PHANTOMS TO LITTLE MILLIONAIRES
MILLIONAIRES ARE PHANTOMS TO US.
THE PENIS IS A PHANTOM FINGER TO A LITTLE GIRL
BREASTS ARE TWIN PHANTOM GOBLETS
PERFECT SUCCESS IS A PHANTOM
PERFECT REVENGE IS A PHANTOM
EVERYONE IN THE NEWSPAPERS AND MAGAZINES IS
A PHANTOM
OTHER PEOPLE IN YOUR BUILDING ARE PHANTOMS
TO THE ARTIST A BIG COLLECTOR IS A PHANTOM
A BIG ARTIST IS A PHANTOM TO A LITTLE GALLERIST
PHANTOMS ARE THE UNKOWN (BUT KNOWN)
THE KITCHEN OF THE RESTAURANT EMPLOYS PHANTOMS
PHANTOMS DRIVE TAXIS
A PHANTOM APPEARS THROUGH KNOWN WALLS
PHANTOMS ARE MASTERS OF OSMOSIS
JOE JONES MAKES PHANTOM MUSIC
NAM JUNE PAIK MAKES PHANTOM TV STRUCTURES
DESIATO MAKES PHANTOM DESECRATIONS
GEOFF HENDRIKS MAKES PHANTOM RITUALS
TOTO IS A PHANTOM OF PHANTOMS

THERE ARE PHANTOM OBJECTS IN ALL THE
MAGAZINES.

NOT ONLY PAIK DOES PHANTOM VIDEO.

WHEN WE DREAM WE ARE PHANTOMS IN THE
DREAM WORLD.

FOR MANY HAPPINESS IS A PHANTOM

FOR MANY POVERTY AND HORROR ARE PHANTOMS

TO CRIMINALS, GETTING CAUGHT BY POLICE
IS PHANTOMIC

PHANTOMS ARE SUPERIOR

PHANTOMS ARE UNIMAGINABLY STRONG

PHANTOMS ARE INEXORABLE

PHANTOMS MAKE NO SENSE

YOU CANNOT DOUBLETHINK PHANTOMS

PHANTOMS ALWAYS WIN

THE PEOPLE WHO ACTUALLY CONTROL THE WORLD ARE
PHANTOMS

SCENE: (DANIEL SPOERRI IS INTRODUCED TO
MARCEL DUCHAMP IN A RESTAURANT)

DANIEL: "PLEASED TO MEET YOU..."

MARCEL: "SO, YOU ARE ONE OF THESE PEOPLE WHO ARE
USING MY IDEAS... " I HAVE
HEARD ABOUT
YOU..."

DANIEL: IF WE WEREN'T USING THESE IDEAS MAYBE
NO ONE WOULD KNOW ABOUT YOU...

BEPPE MORRA MAKES PHANTOM DEALS AND PLANS

DANIEL SPOERRI MAKES PHANTOM BOXES AND
TOPOGRAPHICAL PHANTOM
CONSTELLATIONS OF
PHANTOM OBJECTS.

AL HANSEN IS A PHANTOM ALWAYS A BIT BEYOND

ISTITUTO NAPOLITAN DE CULTURA IS A PHANTOM
ORGANIZATION

THE ULTIMATE AKADEMIE IN COLONIA IS A PHANTOM
CULTURAL INSTITUTION

THE PERFECT LOVE AFFAIR IS A PHANTOM SITUATION

TO THE WOMAN WITH A HUGE VAGINA THE
MAN HUNG LIKE A HORSE IS A PHANTOM

TO THE MAN WITH A TINY COCK LILLIPUT WOMEN
ARE PHANTOMS

AL HANSEN IS A PHANTOM PERFECT LOVER

HIS LIPS BREATHE SOFT KISSES TO THE SPICY
RECTUMS OF ALL THE PHANTOM WOMEN
HE IS ATTRACTED TO

QUOTE: "I SEE A PHANTOM WOMAN AT LEAST ONCE
A WEEK. SOMETHING IN THE WAY SHE WALKS....
I IMAGINE HER HOLDING HER BUTTOCKS APART—
AS I KISS AND LICK, SHE MOANS: ECCO, ECCO, ECCO

LOOK AT THE PHANTOM OBJECTS IN THE SHOP
                                                WINDOWS!

SEE THE PHANTOM SITUATIONS IN THE STREETS.

A LIGHTED WINDOW LATE AT NIGHT INDICATES
                                        A PHANTOM ROOM

EVEN A PHANTOM HOME...

I OBSERVE THE PERFECT STRONG BEHINDS OF
                THE WOMEN OF NAPOLI
QUIVERING STRONG MOUNTAINS JUTTING OVER
            KISSABLE PHANTOM LADY RECTUMS
THE EYE OF THE PHANTOM ~~VOLANGE~~
                        VOLCANO
THE PERFECT LOVER IS A PHANTOM

THE PHANTOMS ARE INTRUDING THROUGH "UNIQUE
            PERSONAL TO THEM" AUREOLES.
THE PHANTOMS OBSERVE US FROM A PHANTOM SPACE
    A PHANTOM POSITION
PHANTOM OBSERVATION POSTS.
THE PHANTOMS ARE NOT HOLY.
HOLLYWOOD IS A PHANTOM PLACE.
ULTIMA THULE IS A PHANTOM HARBOR

                        Al Hansen Napoli
                        1990

ART

1. FIRST, I SEE ART AS A MAGIC ACT. DANCE, THEATER, MUSIC, POETRY, SCULPTURE, PAINTING ALL BEGAN A MILLION OR MORE YEARS AGO AS MAGIC AND CONSTANT PRACTICE OF MAGIC PRODUCED THE BEGINNINGS OF SCIENCE FROM COLLECTED OBSERVATIONS OF NATURAL PHENOMENA. THE FAMILY BECAME THE PACK, THEN CLANS AND TRIBES GREW TO BE CONSIDERED PEOPLES AND NOW, FAIRLY RECENTLY AS NATIONS AND REPUBLICS. THERE ARE STILL QUITE A FEW KINGDOMS AROUND THE WORLD. SO, OVER TIME ART HAS BECOME SEPERATED FROM ITS ORIGINAL FUNCTION. ITS ORIGINAL FUNCTIONS CAMBE SEEN, VESTIGIALLY IF NOT IN MANY CASES, COMPLETELY IN THE ART THAT IS PART OF THE MAGIC AND RELIGION OF BUSHMEN IN AFRICA, AUSTRALIAN ABORIGINES, SIBERIAN SHAMANS, AMAZON TRIBES AND THE MUD MEN AND OTHER TRIBES OF NEW GUINEA.

WRITTEN HISTORY HAS BEEN HAPPENING FOR JUST A FEW THOUSAND YEARS. THE ORIGINAL PEOPLE OF RUSSIA WERE ASTONISHED TO FIND THAT THE VIKINGS COULD MAKE MARKS ON PAPER AND THAT FIFTY OR A HUNDRED MILES AWAY ANOTHER NORSEMAN WOULD LOOK AT THE MARKS AND THEN ASSEMBLE A PACKAGE OF 2 DOZEN EGGS, 3 KILOS OF BUTTER, AND ½ KILO OF LARD. WE CAN GET IDEAS OF PREHISTORY BY READING HOW HISTORY BEGAN. AND IN ABOUT THE YEARS 750-800 (I AM VAGUE ON EXACT DATES) THAT

IS HOW RUSSIAN HISTORY BEGINS. WE KNOW THERE
WERE LONG ICE AGES. NAM JUNE PAIK SAYS THAT
DURING THE ICE AGES THERE WAS NO SUN ONLY
THE MOON. MAKES SENSE.

2. SECONDLY, IT IS MY DEEPLY FELT BELIEF THAT
ART-MAKING IS A BUILT-IN, PSYCHO-SOCIAL CULTURAL
IMPERATIVE. I SEE ART-MAKING AS A FABRIC WOVEN
OVER TIME, CONTINUOUSLY SINCE THE BEGINNINGS OF
PEOPLE KIND. ON THE FIRST CHRISTMAS DAY THERE WERE
ABOUT 250,000,000 PEOPLE IN THE WORLD. SIXTEEN CENTURIES
LATER WHEN THE ENGLISH AND DUTCH PILGRIMS LANDED AT
PLYMOUTH ROCK, IN MASSACHUSETTS THE WORLD POPULATION
HAD DOUBLED TO 500,000,000. BY THE LATE 1700'S WHEN
THE AMERICAN DECLARATION OF INDEPENCE WAS CREATED
THE WORLD POPULATION WAS 700,000,000. BY 1931 WHEN
ALDOUS HUXLEY WROTE 'BRAVE NEW WORLD' IT WAS 2,000,800,000.
ABOUT 50,000,000 A YEAR INCREASE. PEOPLE KIND INCREASES
EVERY FOUR YEARS BY ABOUT 255 AND A HALF MILLION. THAT IS
THE POPULATION OF THE U.S. EVERY 8½ YEARS WORLD POP-
ULATION INCREASES BY 860 AND A HALF MILLIONS. THAT IS
THE POPULATION OF INDIA. FROM THE BIRTH OF CHRIST TO THE
DEATH OF QUEEN ELIZABETH I IT TOOK 16 CENTURIES FOR
THE POPULATION OF EARTH TO DOUBLE. AT THE PRESENT RATE
IT DOUBLES AT LESS THAN 50 YEARS, LESS THAN HALF A
CENTURY!
    AS RECENTLY AS 1950 THERE WERE 53,000,000 MOTOR CARS
REGISTERED IN THE WORLD. BY 1992 WELL OVER HALF A BILLION
CARS AND TRUCKS WERE REGISTERED AND BEFORE THE YEAR
2000 IT WILL BE A FULL BILLION.
    SO, ONE HAS THE ICE AGE RECEDING AND PEOPLE COMING OUT OF
THEIR CAVES AND FORAGING FOR FOOD. NOMAD TRAILS BECOME TRADE
ROUTES, TRADE ROUTE CROSSING POINTS BECOMING VILLAGES, TOWNS

AND BEGINNING CITIES. OVER THESE THOUSANDS OF YEARS ONE HAS THE CONSTANT DEVELOPMENT OF WAYS OF MAKING THINGS AND COMING TO TERMS WITH HOW THE WORLD SEEMS TO WORK AND TRYING TO CONTROL IT OR HANDLE IT THROUGH MAGIC, RELIGION AND MUDDLING AND COPING. THE DEVELOPMENT OF TRAVOIS, TO CARTS, TO WAGONS AND COACHES AND FINALLY STEAM, OIL, GAS, ELECTRICITY, BROADCASTING THEN TELE-VISION AND COMPUTERS AND FAX. AND OVER THESE YEARS A CERTAIN NUMBER OF PEOPLE ARE NEEDED TO BE BAKERS, BUS DRIVERS, BUS AND AUTO MECHANICS, DOCTORS, NURSES, JOURNALISTS, PRINTERS, FARMERS, VETERINARIANS, SAILORS, CARPENTERS... AND INTERESTINGLY ENOUGH, IT IS OBVIOUS THAT THERE HAS BEEN A NEED, IN THE PSYCHO-SOCIAL COMMUNITIES OF PEOPLE KIND, FOR A CERTAIN NUMBER OF PEOPLE TO BECOME ARTISTS. ARTISANS, (HANDWERKEN) DESIGNED AND MADE TOOLS, SHOES, WEAPONS, CUPS, GLASSES, DISHES, EATING IMPLEMENTS, PEOPLE MADE THEIR OWN CANDLES. ART AS WE KNOW IT TODAY DIDN'T EXIST. UP UNTIL THE QUATTROCENTO ART WAS INVOLVED WITH RELIGION. ABOUT 11 OR 1200 LAWS BEGAN TO BE CODIFIED IN BOLOGNA AND THE MIDDLE PERSON POPULATION BEGINNING IN THE MIDDLE AGES BEGAN TO GROW. THE BOURGOISIE.

A CENTRAL PROBLEM FOR ART PEOPLE IS THE SPLIT BETWEEN ARTS AND CRAFTS. WEAVING, CERAMICS, GLASSBLOWING ARE SEEN AS MAKING THINGS TO BE USED WHILE PAINTINGS ARE DECORATION. SOMETHING NOT REALLY NEEDED IN A HOUSE OR BUILDING. CRAFT PEOPLE MAKE THINGS THAT FUNCTION. MANY OF US DO NOT SEE THAT THE FUNCTION OF AN ARTWORK IS TO DEVELOP ONE'S ABILITY TO FEEL TO COMMUNICATE AND EXPERIENCE NON-VERBALLY. AND EVERY KIND OF PICTURE OR ARTWORK CAN BE AND IS USED BY EVERYONE. THE MAJORITY OF PEOPLE DO THIS UNCONSCIOUSLY. AFTER ONLY A BRIEF TIME, PERHAPS FOR ONLY ONE OR TWO MONTHS BACK THERE AS THE MIDDLEMAN BOURGOISIE CAME INTO BEING THERE BECAME ART DEALERS, KUNSTHANDEL AND AFTER PERHAPS TWO HUNDRED YEARS GALLERIES BEGAN. WITHIN THE ELITES THAT CONTROLLED WHATEVER WAS THOUGHT TO BE THE TOP ART

OF THE TIME THERE DEVELOPED PEOPLE WHO WOULD BE
GOOD AT EXPLAINING OR APPRECIATING WORK. THUS, THE
ART CRITIC COMES INTO BEING. WHY SHOULD YOU BUY THIS AND
NOT THIS. ALL THIS VERBALIZING ABOUT ART INCREASES, IN
EXPONENTIAL LOG, THE NON-VERBAL POSSIBILITIES, AND POTENTIAL FOR FEELING,
FOR DEVELOPING THE ABILITY TO FEEL BY LOOKING AT AND COMM-
UNICATING WITH ART. THE MODERN WORK OF ART IS NOT ABOUT
HOW ANY THING LOOKS. IT IS UNTO ITSELF. IT IS. IT IS AN IDEA.
MORE THAN A REPRESENTATION OF AN OBSERVATION. COMMUNISTS
HAD A PROBLEM ABOUT THE ROLE OF MODERN ART IN THE CLASS
STRUGGLE. BECAUSE EACH PERSON SEES WHAT THEY SEE INDIVID-
UALLY THERE IS A POINTING UP OR AN ACCENT ON INDIVIDUALISM.
AND WHAT COMMUNISM, ~~BECAME~~ WHICH IS STILL A VERY GOOD IDEA,
HAD BECOME USED FOR FOUND INDIVIDUALISM VERY DANGEROUS.
SO DID THE CZARS, AND SO DOES (OR DID) THE CATHOLIC CHURCH.
AND ISLAM. EVERYONE STAY IN YOUR PLACE AND DON'T ROCK
THE BOAT. LET THE LEADERS APPROVED BY THE RICH LEAD AND
THE RICH GET RICHER AND THE POOR GET MORE AND MORE
TELEVISION CHANNELS EACH YEAR.

I WON'T GO INTO CRITICS AT ALL. IN FACT, I THINK I COVERED THAT.

THIRDLY THERE ARE GALLERIES AND GALLERISTS AND KUNST-
HANDEL AND HOW SUCCESSFUL THEY ARE CAN BE SEEN IN THE
FACT THAT AUCTION HOUSES COME INTO BEING TO HANDLE THE
HUNDRED'S OF YEARS PROFIT OF ALL THE DIFFERENT ARTS AND
CRAFTS AND NOW (WHERE ARE YOU WALTER BENJAMIN WHEN WE
NEED YOU?) COLLECTIBLE/NOSTALGIA ITEMS FROM EVERY DAY LIFE.
I CONSIDER IT AN INTERESTING PROOF THAT ART IS NOT SUPPOSED
TO HAVE ANY THING TO DO WITH MONEY IS THE FACT THAT ALL
ARTISTS AS THEY BEGIN TO SELL OR HAVE THE FIRST OPPORTUNITIES
TO SELL, FIND IT IMPOSSIBLE OR VERY, VERY HARD TO SAY HOW MUCH

MONEY THE ARTWORK IS WORTH. USUALLY IT IS A FAIRLY LOW PRICE. ANOTHER PROOF OF THE PSYCHO-SOCIAL CULTURAL IMPERATIVE IS THAT AT THE BEGINNING OF LIFE ABSOLUTELY EVERYONE IS AN ART MAKER! AT THE BEGINNING IT IS JUST PURE EXPRESSION. THEN AFTER KINDERGARTEN AND EARLY SCHOOL BEGINS THE RULER, NEATNESS AND THEMES/SUBJECTS ARE DICTATED. AS WE BECOME TEENAGERS MOST OF US STOP DOING ART A LOT. ITS IMPORTANT, YOU SEE, THAT THERE ARE ENOUGH NURSES, BUS MECHANICS, AIR PLANE PILOTS, BAKERS, POLICE, FIREMEN, DENTISTS ETC. EVEN IN PREHISTORIC TIMES ONE ONLY NEEDED A FEW ARTISTS. IF ART HADNT BECOME DETACHED OR UNHOOKED FROM ITS ORIGINAL FUNCTION THERE WOULDNT BE AS MANY NEEDED AS THERE ARE NOW UNDER THE NEW, MODERN, PRESENT CONDITIONS. LOOK AT THE PROBLEMS IN ENGLAND WITH ALL THE COAL MINERS WHEN THE POLITICAL ELITE HAS A BIG INVESTMENT IN (AND OWNS) NATURAL GAS. HAVE THE MINERS CLEAN THEIR FINGERNAILS AND TAKE COMPUTER TRAINING? AND MOST GALERISTS, DURING MOMENTS OF LUCIDITY, WILL SAY "I HAVE ABSOLUTELY NO IDEA HOW OR WHY I AM IN THIS BUSINESS!" IT IS QUITE NORMAL FOR A PERSON TO OPEN AN ART GALLERY WITHOUT ANY EXPERIENCE AT ALL. ONLY A SMALL NUMBER OF GALLERISTS HAVE DEGREES IN ART HISTORY FOR EXAMPLE AND AN EVEN MUCH SMALLER NUMBER WORKED IN GALLERIES FOR SOME YEARS BEFORE OPENING THEIR OWN GALLERIES. THE CULTURAL IMPERATIVE NEEDS PEOPLE TO BECOME GALLERISTS BECAUSE THERE ARE ALWAYS MORE ARTISTS WHO CANNOT FIND A GALLERY. MANY YOUNG ARTISTS FORM COOPERATIVE GALLERIES AND PERFORMANCE SPACES.

BUT IT IS INTERESTING AND ANOTHER PROOF OF MY PSYCHO-SOCIAL CULTURAL IMPERATIVE THAT ARTISTS HAVE A PROBLEM ABOUT PRICING THEIR WORK. NOW, IN NATURE A BIRD

CAN'T FLY AROUND WITH AN EGG IN IT. SO BIRDS DO AN
INTERESTING THING. THEY EXTERNALIZE THE WOMB INTO
A NEST. THE EGGS GO THERE AND THEY TAKE TURNS SITTING
ON THE EGGS ~~SO~~ SO THEY ARE WARM AND THEY TAKE TURNS
FEEDING EACH OTHER. SO, WITHIN THE FRAMEWORK OF MY
PSYCHO-SOCIAL CULTURAL IMPERATIVE THE ARTIST EXTERNALIZES
THE NEED TO PRICE ITS WORK AND THE PSCI REGULARLY
SENDS OUT A SIGNAL AND ONE MORE PERSON SUDDENLY DECIDES
TO OPEN AN ART GALLERY. LIKE SO MUCH OF LIFE IT IS A
RANDOM CHANCE OPERATION THAT ONLY HALF WORKS.
BUT IT WORKS.

FOURTH, COMES THE 20TH CENTURY AND MODERN ART
AND THE IDEA OF AN AVANT GARDE. EARLY IN THE 1900'S THERE
APPEARED THE FIRST ABSTRACT PAINTING. THE FIRST NON-
REPRESENTATIONAL ARTWORK. THERE IS SOME WEIGHT IN
SUPPORT OF FRANCIS PICABIA AND THERE ARE ONE OR TWO
OTHERS BUT I REMEMBER, AS A YOUNG ARTIST IN GREENWICH
VILLAGE IN NEW YORK CITY IN THE LATE FORTIES, AN OLDER
ARTIST TOLD ME THAT WHEN HE WAS YOUNG IN THE TWENTIES
HE HAD A TEACHER WHO HAD BEEN YOUNG IN THE 1890'S
AND 1900'S IN PARIS. THIS OLDER ARTISTS OPINION OF
ABSTRACT PAINTING WAS, "THAT IT WAS ALRIGHT TO DO
'COLOR STUDIES' IN THE STUDIO BUT ONE DIDN'T SHOW THEM
IN A GALLERY AS ART. SO, IN TERMS OF MY SEEING ART
AS A CONTINUOUS FABRIC, A CONSTANT FLOWING OF
ALWAYS CHANGING AND FLUXING WAYS OF EXPRESSION,
I WONDER IF RAPHAEL DA SANZIO AND MICHELANGELO
BUONAROTTI DID NOT DO COLOR STUDIES. IN EVERY STUDIO
GOING BACK TO MONASTERYS THERE HAVE BEEN CAKED UP
COLOR ON ARTISTS PALETTES. TO ME THESE ARE GORGEOUS.

TO ME, MODERN AVANT-GARDE ART BEGINS WITH GUILLAUME APPOLINAIRES 'WORLD POEM' WHICH IS LIKE A WIDE SCROOL RATHER THAN AN A-4 PAGE WITH LINES FLUSH LEFT SO THERE IS NOT A SET WAY TO READ IT IT IS LIKE A WEATHER MAP OF WORDS AND PHRASES AND IT FREES POETRY FROM FORMS SUCH AS THE ODE, SONNET, COUPLET, CELESTINA, ETC. IT 'FEELS' ENVIRONMENTAL. I THINK IT IS FROM BEFORE THE 1900'S. 1890 SOMETHING PERHAPS.

ABOUT THIS TIME ALFRED JARRY WROTE HIS PATAPHYSICS PAPERS. THIS WAS A VERY FRENCH ZEN PHILOSOPHY THAT I FEEL PREFIGURED DADA THINKING EARLY AND FLUXUS LATER. THE SENSE IN NONSENSE AND THE NONSENSE IN SO-CALLED SENSIBLE DISCOURSES. FOR EXAMPLE, THE AVERAGE NEWSPAPER WHICH MARSHALL MACLUHAN SAW AS AN X-RAY OF A SOCIETY.

THE MOST IMPORTANT 20TH CENTURY ARTIST FOR ME IS JOHN CAGE BECAUSE HE BROUGHT TOGETHER, OR WAS A THINKING COLLAGE OF MAHOLY-NAGY, MARCEL DUCHAMP AND BUCKMINSTER FULLER AND ZEN BHUDDISM. IN ANOTHER SENSE KURT SCHWITTERS AND MATISSE ARE IMPORTANT TO MY MIXED MEDIA COLLAGE AND ASSEMBLAGE WORKS. SO SCHWITTERS TAKING TRASH CAN PAPERS AND COLLAGING THEM IS QUITE AN ASPECT OR VIBRATION FROM OR WITH JOHN CAGE'S GROWING ATTRACTION AND COMMITMENT TO ENVIRONMENTAL AND CHANCE OPERATION SOUND AS A WAY OF EGOLESSLY COMPOSING MUSIC. AT BLACK MOUNTAIN COLLEGE, NORTH CAROLINA HE, MERCE CUNNINGHAM AND OTHERS DID NON LINEAR FREE FORM HAPPENINGS OF UNRELATED ACTS, EVENTS, SOUNDS, AND SITUATIONS, SO THE FIRST HAPPENINGS IN AMERICA WERE DONE BY JOHN CAGE (IN THE LATE 40'S EARLY FIFTIES) ALLAN KAPROW COMES LATER, ACTUALLY OSKAR SCHLEMMER IN HIS BAUHAUS

THEATRE MANIFESTO (LATE TWENTIES-EARLY THIRTIES?) SAYS
"LET THERE BE A THEATER OF HAPPENINGS, SITUATIONS AND EVENTS."
SO MUCH FOR ACTION ART, PERFORMANCE, FLUXUS EVENTS, U.a.!
KAPROW DEVELOPED A RITUAL APPROACH TO AKTION ART
QUITE DIFFERENT FROM HERMANN NITSCH. KAPROW'S ARE
DRY, NITSCHES ORGIES ARE QUITE RICHLY WET, WITH BLOOD,
MILK, WATER AND HONEY. THE DIFFERENCE BETWEEN THEM IS
THAT KAPROWS ARE NON-VERBAL WHILE NITSCH IS QUITE
DIDACTIC. SIMPLY, IF MEN ARE ATTRACTED TO THE GORE OF
WAR THEN WHY NOT EXPERIENCE THIS AS A RITUAL AND
NOT FIGHT WARS.

ONE OF SEVERAL MAJOR ASPECTS OF JOHN CAGE'S ART CAN
BE SEEN FROM THE FOLLOWING:

IN MAHOLY NAGY'S BOOK THE NEW VISION, THERE IS A CIRCLE DES-
CRIBING THE INDIVIDUAL. IT SHOWS THAT EACH
INDIVIDUAL IS CAPABLE OF DOING ANYTHING A HUMAN
BEING NEEDS TO DO. THROUGH CIRCUMSTANCES WE BE-
COME SPECIALISTS INSTEAD OF WHOLE PEOPLE.

1ST CHANGE IN MUSIC WAS THRU CHANCE OPERATIONS
TO MAKE A MUSIC IN WHICH HE WOULD NOT EXPRESS
HIS FEELINGS OR IDEAS, BUT MUSIC IN WHICH THE SOUNDS
THEMSELVES WOULD CHANGE HIM. THEY WOULD CHANGE
HIS LIKES & DISLIKES, HE WOULD FIND THRU USING
CHANCE OPERATIONS THAT THINGS HE THOUGHT HE
DISLIKED, HE ACTUALLY LIKED. RATHER THAN BECOMING
A MORE AND MORE REFINED MUSICIAN HE WOULD BECOME
MORE AND MORE RECEPTIVE TO THE VARIOUS POSSIBILITIES
OF SOUND. HIS INDIVIDUAL PREFERENCE IN TERMS OF MUSICAL AESTHETIC
EXPERIENCE IS NOT HIS MUSIC AND NOT THE MUSIC OF
ANY OTHER COMPOSER BUT RATHER THE SOUNDS AND NOISES
OF EVERYDAY LIFE. ALL THE PARAMETERS OF MUSIC ARE
LARGER IN ENVIRONMENTAL SOUND THAN IN ORGANIZED
MUSIC SOUNDS.
MARCEL DUCHAMP SAID," THE HUMAN MIND WORKS VERY
POORLY, PARTICULARLY WHEN IT IS INVOLVED WITH ORGANIZATION
BECAUSE ONLY THE SIMPLEST POSSIBILITIES SEEM TO
FASCINATE THE ORGANIZING MIND. JOHN CAGES WHOLE
THRUST WAS TO FREE MUSIC FROM THE CLUTCHES OF THE
a,b,a. EUROPEAN MUSIC JUST USES A TINY NUMBER
OF THE POSSIBILITIES FOR STRUCTURING SOUND. IF YOU
LISTEN TO ENVIRONMENTAL SOUND YOU ARE CONTINUALLY
STRUCK BY THE BRILLIANCE OF NON ORGANIZATION.

THRU CHANCE OPERATIONS HE BECAME MORE OPEN TO HIS LIFE EXPERIENCE. HE CHANGED HIMSELF. HE BECAME INTERESTED IN INDETERMINACY. FROM 1954 TO 1958 IN BONN AND DARMSTADT HE BEGAN TO INCLUDE X IN HIS PARTITUREN TO SIGNIFY ANYTHING OR SOMETHING NOT THOUGHT OF AT ALL (BY THE COMPOSER) THIS GAVE A FREEDOM TO THE INDIVIDUAL PERFORMER AND THIS BEGAN TO INTEREST JOHN CAGE MORE AND MORE. GIVING THIS FREEDOM TO MUSICIANS LIKE DAVID TUDOR, GORDON MUMMA, DAVID BERMAN, ALVIN LUCIER, ETC. IT PROVIDED RESULTS THAT WERE EXTRAORDINARILY BEAUTIFUL. WHERE THIS FREEDOM IS GIVEN TO PEOPLE WHO ARE NOT DISCIPLINED, WHO DO NOT START FROM ZERO (THE ABSENCE OF LIKES AND DISLIKES) WHO ARE NOT CHANGED INDIVIDUALS, BUT WHO REMAIN PEOPLE WITH PARTICULAR LIKES AND DISLIKES, THEN THE GIVING OF FREEDOM IS OF NO INTEREST. BUT WHEN THIS FREEDOM IS GIVEN TO DISCIPLINED PEOPLE THEN ONE SEES AN INSTANCE OF A SOCIETY THAT HAS CHANGED. NOT AN INDIVIDUAL BUT A GROUP OF INDIVIDUALS AND YOU SHOW THE PRACTICALITY OF ANARCHY. ANARCHY IN THE SENSE OF A GROUP OF PEOPLE ACTING WITHOUT ANY ONE OF THEM TELLING ALL OF THEM WHAT TO DO.

SO FROM THE ANARCHY OF GUILLAUME APPOLLINAIRE'S "WORLD POEM" TO JOHN CAGE'S MEISTER ECKEHART ZEN.

Al Hansen   KÖLN 1993

Sie

AL HANSEN
1927-1995

EARLY BACKGROUND
1927 Born in Richmond Hill, Queens, New York
1945 Military Service, 82nd Airborne Division, Frankfurt, Cologne
1948 Berlin, Germany.
1950 US Airforce, Tactical Air Command
1954 South Carolina

EDUCATION
1949 Art Students League, New York City - John Groth
1950 Brooklyn College - Al Terris
1956 New School For Social Research - Experimental Music
      - John Cage
1959 Pratt Institute
1963 Environmental Loft Studio and Mixed Media Event Studies

TEACHING HISTORY
1967-74 Rutgers University, Newark, New Jersey
1970 Parsons School of Design
1979 Eskimo Art School. Nuuk-G., Greenland
1987 Founded the "Ultimate Akademie" with Lisa Cieslik,
      Cologne
1988 Hochschule fur Bildende Kunst. Hamburg

SOLO EXHIBITIONS\EDITIONS
HIGHLIGHTS
1960 New York 6 Gallery. Watercolors, New York
1961 New York Walking Show, New York
1964 Judson Gallery, New York
1966 Eastend Gallery, Massachussetts
1967 Ringelhaupt Gallery, Boston
      Hallmark Gallery, New York
1970 Galerie Block, Berlin
      Galerie Ingo Kummel, Cologne
1972 Galerie Inge Baecker, Bochum
1974 Galerie der Spiegel. Archive Show, Cologne
1979 "Collage and Construction," Galerie A, Amsterdam, Holland
      Henie Museum. Oslo
      Royal Academy of Art, Copenhagen
1980 Munchatelier, Kultusministerium, Oslo
1981 Edition and Galerie Hundertmark. "Black Book,"
      Cologne
      Karl Valentin Museum. Munich
1982 Galerie Petersom Berlin
1986 "Structures and Sculptures," Galerie Offermann,
      Cologne
      "In Search of the Goddess," Gracie Mansion Gallery,
      New York
      Zeichnungen, Aquerelle. "Andy Warhol Attentat,"
      Edition Hundertmark, Cologne, Germany
1988 "Collagen, Objekte, Fingerbilder," Galerie Klewan, Munich
      Gracie Mansion Gallery, New York
1989 Artothek Koln, Cologne, Germany
      Galerie Kolon, Cologne, Germany
      Gracie Mansion Gallery, New York
1990 "The Temple Of The Goddess," Galerie Kolon, Cologne

1991 Galerie Klewan, Munich
      "Exposition," Galerie 1900-2000 Marcel Fleiss, Paris
1992 Lisi Hamerle Gallery, Bregenz, Austria
1993 Galerie Klewan, Munich
1994 Troy Gallery, Los Angeles
1995 Michael Wewerka Gallery, Berlin
      Gracie Mansion Gallery, New York
      Kunstverein Rosenheim, Rosenheim
1996 Kölnisches Stadt Museum, Cologne

GROUP SHOWS
1959 "Below Zero," with Rauschenberg, Oldenburg, Dine, Kaprow,
      Reuben Gallery, New York
1960 "Ray Gun Spex," with Kaprow, Dine, Oldenburg, Judson
      Gallery (Hansen: Multiple Projections), New York
1963 "Fluxus Anti-Musik Festival," with Beuys, Hansen, Paik, and
      Spoerri, Staatliche Kunstakademie. Dusseldorf
1966 "Juxtapositionen," Neue Galerie, Aachen
1969 "Happening & Fluxus," Kolnischer Kunstverein, Cologne
1970 "This Is Not Here Show," with Yoko Ono and John Lennon,
      Everson Museum, Syracuse, New York.
1973 Berlin, "Phenomenatransactionskunst:
      A Hansen Mini- Retrospective," Galerie Block
1975 Bochum. "Collage/Decollage Works by
      Brecht, Filliou, Hansen, Schwitters, Spoerri, Vostell,
      Watts and others," Galerie Baecker.
1977 Berlin. "Photographie Exhibition. Works by:
      Beuys, Duchamp, Baumgarten, Becher, Hansen, Hodicke,
      Kaprow, Knoebel," Galerie Block.
1982 "Attersee Party Performance," with Beuys, Rot,
      Lupertz, Attersee, Wurthie, Iannone in der Exil Bar,
      Kreuzberg, Berlin
1984 "Gruppenausstel" With Hansen, Cieslik and Yilmaz, Cologne
1986 "Unausgewogen." Kölnischer Kunstverein. Cologne, Germany
1987 "Conflux-Ausstellung." Wewerka Galerie, Berlin
1988 "Mobel als Kunstobjekt." Kunstlerwerkstatt. Munich
      Parallel, Dokumentas Banana, Erotica, Fotografica Ultimate
      Akademie, Ausstellungen, Cologne
1989 "The Junk Aesthetic" Whitney Museum, New York
      "Happening & Fluxus" Galerie 1900 2000, Paris
      "Walk Don't Walk" Walkman Show, Kunstlerbuch Galerie,
      Cologne
1992 "Fluxus-Virus" Cologne Kuntsverein, Cologne
      "L'Art Est Inutile" Bregenzer Kunstverein, Palais Thurm und
      Taxis, Bregenz, Austria
1994 Group Show, Copenhagen, Denmark, With Hansen, Gyr, Den
      Fria ,Galerie Mamus, With Henryk Pryds Beck,
      Copenhagen
1995 Fluxus Virus, With Hansen and Ben Patterson, St. Petersberg
      and Moscow
      "Pasted Papers" Collage in the 20th Century" Louis Stern
      Gallery, Los Angeles
      "The Gun: Icon of Twenthieth Century Art", UBU Gallery,
      New York
1996 Fotouhi Cramer Gallery, "Box", New York
      "Aus der Sammlung" Rafael Vostell Fine Art, Berlin
1998 "Out of Actions", Museum of Contemporary Art, Los Angeles
      "Beck and Al Hansen, Playing with Matches", Santa Monica
      Museum of Art, Los Angeles; Thread Waxing Space,
      New York; Plug In, Winnipeg.

BECK
1970-

Beck Hansen was born and raised in Los Angeles and started playing an acoustic guitar as a teenager. Inspired initially by American folk music and Delta Blues, Beck immersed himself in the music of Fred McDowell, Woody Guthrie and others from the folk and blues tradition. But it wasn't until he moved to New York and happened upon the East Village anti-folk scene that he found his true calling. Sadly, the anti-folk scene of the late 1980s was not well documented. It combined a punk aesthetic with a roots style, freeing folk music from its clichéd 1960s protest chains. Anti-folk made Beck realize there are no restrictions when it comes to subject matter for songs. It was this discovery that set him on his current course in music.

Beck's early LA performances were usually wedged between sets by his friends' bands. Most of the time he'd play at Raji's, Al's Bar or parties - wherever something was happening. In 1991 he met then-fledgling hip-hop producer Karl Stephenson. Together they began recording the material that would comprise *Mellow Gold*. Beck's continued adventures in sound have resulted in extensive touring and the critically acclaimed *Odelay*, another trip to the sonic frontier, starting with folk music and spreading out - in all directions.

While growing up in LA, Beck was encouraged by his mother, Bibbe Hansen, to draw and write. He later produced a literary and art magazine called *Youthless*. He attended art gallery openings and performance events and met artists involved in the marginal underground music and art scenes. His grandfather, Al Hansen, was a strong influence on his understanding of what art could be and what role it played in society. Their early discussions left an immediate impact and informed Beck's magazine design, collages, assemblages and concepts about merging visual art with sound and words.

SELECTED DISCOGRAPHY

Mellow Gold, DGC, 1994.
Stereopathic Soulmanure, Flipside, 1994.
One Foot in the Grave, K, 1994.
Odelay, DGC, 1996.

AWARDS

1996-97 Grammy Awards for "Where It's At" - best male vocal rock performance and best alternative music performance. Grammy nomination for album of the year. Artist of the year - *SPIN* magazine, *Rolling Stone* Critic's Poll. Album of the year - *Rolling Stones* Critic's Poll and Reader's Poll, *Los Angeles Times* Critic's Poll, Neil Strauss & Jon Pareles (New York Times), *Request Magazine* Critic's Poll. Worldwide Artist of the Year, *NME*. *Odelay* - No. 1 Album of the Year, CMJ.

ACKNOWLEDGEMENTS

Beck & Al Hansen: Playing With Matches started with a dinner in New York among, Sean Carrillo, Jackie Ox, Jon Hendricks, Larry Miller and myself at Joe Jones' old avant-garde hang out, the Ear Bar on the Lower West Side. Sean mentioned a great many things that evening about Fluxus and Happenings artists and events, and the Al Hansen Archive in Los Angeles. He was in New York collecting artwork and papers belonging to his father-in-law, Al Hansen, who died sitting in a favourite chair in his studio on Kysshauserstrasse in June, 1995. He left a paper chase of ephemera, letters, notes, books, documentation and artwork in 11 or 12 different media in several countries. Sean was wading through the New York material in close touch with his partner and colleague, Bibbe Hansen, Al's only daughter. After discussing the finer details of Al's relationship to all kinds of refuse, it occurred to me that Beck Hansen, Al's grandson, was following in his grandfather's footsteps, excavating new but not dissimilar terrain with high and low technology and a mass audience in tow. I was immediately interested in their shared approaches to artistic production. Al joked about the "old school" artist's studio and using live models while in reality he was more likely to commandeer a bar room, molding elements of its contents and clientele and his performative actions into his assemblages. I wanted to explore the visible objects and speculate on evidence of the immaterial vitality generated by each artist. When combined, these objects/images and performative actions established a sophisticated base in languaging.

My chance meeting sparked research visits to Los Angeles, Cologne, Verona, New York, Vancouver and other locations to pick up the pieces of the puzzle. To Bibbe Hansen and Sean Carrillo I owe a great deal of gratitude for developing their archive before Al died and for opening the Al Hansen Archive to scrutiny. They understood immediately the importance of Al's little known handwritten texts in the Archive, Al's intermedia poetry full of rhythm, rhymes and recklessness.

In the process of putting together this book (and a related exhibition), others, like Tom Patchett and Susan Martin of Smart Art Press and Track 16 Gallery in LA were important collaborators involved in the graphic design process and all aspects of the exhibition at one time or another. A great deal of support also came from the "miracle chiropractors", Drs. Russell and Mark Baerwaldt in Genoa and Milan. Their inestimable critical and financial support for the book is greatly appreciated. Francesco Conz's archive and collection provided a wealth of material, and the personal relationship that Mr. Conz had with Al since the 1970s yielded insights into not ony Al's materials and techniques, but also his very productive sojourns in the Archive Conz studios in Asolo and Verona. What Francesco Conz realized early on was the crucial importance of collecting and publishing work by intermedia artists linked to Fluxus, Happenings, Zaj, Gutai, Viennese Aktionismus, Lettrisme and other areas of experimentation. Mr. Conz believes that everything an artist touches matters and deserves archival treatment.

Numerous other collectors have contributed to the book, and I am grateful to each one, including Pietro Pellini, Jane Holzer, Dorothy Lichtenstein, Ilene and Michael Salcman, Claes Oldenburg and Coosje Van Bruggen, Peter Hutchinson, Jasper Johns, Jonas Mekas, Idelle and Julian Weber, Buster Cleveland and Diane Sipprelle, Alison Knowles and Gracie Mansion.

I would also like to thank Didi Dunphy and the Board of Directors at the Santa Monica Museum of Art, as well as Thomas Rhoads, Carole Ann Klonarides, Terry Morello and Barbara Jones, for their advice and guidance. Thanks also to Ellen Salpeter and Lia Gangitano at Thread Waxing Space, New York. Pietro Pellini and Yola Berbesz of the Ultimate Akademy, Cologne, and the Kunst-Bild-Archiv, Köln, spent many hours with me reviewing photographs, video and audiotapes (including telephone answering machine tapes), looking for the idiosyncratic audio and videotape I was intent on collecting for Beck's compilation tape. A special thank-you is extended to Hans-Hermann T. in Cologne for making available a series of portraits of Al in his studio, ephemera and for performance video footage. Thank you to Charlie Gross in New York and Dan Winters in LA, Hans-Harmann T. in Cologne, Francesco Conz in Verona, Valerie Herouvis, Jan Van Raay, Michael Broome and Beck for the stunning photographs. Thank you to Heike Hoffmann and Skulli Acosta in Cologne, Joe Wolin, Jon Hendricks, Geoff Hendricks, and Sur Rodney Sur in New York, Plug In Gallery's Board of Directors in Winnipeg, Canada, who all contributed their patience, knowledge and/or materials to develop the project. Thanks also to Shauna O'Brien and John Silva at Gold Mountain and Dennis Dennehy at Geffen Records.

Finally, and without reservation, I would like to thank Susan Chafe for her keen eye, design skills and collaboration; photographers William Eakin, Bill Short, Fabrizio Garghetti, and Sheila Spence for their expert documentation of the art; Alison Gillmor for editing and Rodney LaTourelle for the 'tapping'.

Plug In Editions is grateful for the ongoing support of the Manitoba Arts Council and the Canada Council.

Wayne Baerwaldt

The rooter, the hawk and the phoenix

The McMiracle Continues: A Cool Head Wins a Heated Crapshoot

Bills Find New Way to Pain Raiders: The Boot in Overtime

Monetary milestone on a European two-speed road to ruin

Holiday Bowl Mix, Sweetened by Scandal but Free of Fines, Takes Final Shape

With Israel's Rejection and Syria's Silence, Talks Elude U.S.

Nasal-Spray Treatment Offers Hope to Doomed Cystic Fibrosis Patients

For High Desert Mavericks, Baseball's Songs Are Sweet, if Always in a Minor Key

On the House Gym Floor, Lawmakers Meet but They Don't Pass Much

Japanese market fidgets on verge of recovery

With One Year Left Before the Olympics, Barcelona's Work Is Far From Finished

Down-to-earth space men ready for take-off

Swiss Bank Deregulation Shakes Up the Fortress Mentality

Ritual power of the madding crowd

Falcons Beat Saints on Perfect Day for Underdogs

Running a gauntlet of hardened hearts

US sharks bite British raiders

Sweet charity swinging low

The sound of distant voices

Mortgage plan punches hole in safety net

Piggott loses out in family affair

How to let nothing you dismay

We can help you call your boss in Boston.

State of parties points to hung championship

Kiwis have plenty to Crowe about

The Guru of Miscellaneous Percussion

INTERMEDIA POEM   Al Hansen 1993

SMART READER:

The freewheeling humor of Al Hansen's work and the richness of Beck Hansen's musical experimentation point to one of the core issues in all contemporary art: the reinvigoration and elevation of the mundane and often overlooked elements of everyday life into lyrical and novel forms of creative expression. Smart Art Press is happy to partner with Plug In Editions to bring to light the work of two such singularly talented individuals.

Man Ray
Paris>>L.A.

Softcover, 9 x 12 inches
128 pp
140 color illustrations
$30

The first-ever in-depth look at the life and art of Man Ray during the decade he lived in Southern California (1941–1950), this handsome, illustrated book documents the local color and the colorful personalities that dominated the scene, as well as major paintings, letters, and documents by Man Ray commenting on the movies and life in California.

William S. Burroughs
Concrete and Buckshot

Softcover, $6^1/2$ x 9 inches
50 pp
15 color, 16 b&w illustrations
$15

This book/catalogue focuses on Burroughs's achievement as a painter and includes concrete poetry written by legendary 20th-century philosopher-cum-pop culture guru Timothy Leary shortly before his death. Representing the new generation of artist/writers is Benjamin Weissman's "Sad but Happy," a Burroughs-esque literary adventure into the dark side.

Pierre Molinier

Hardcover, $8^1/2$ x $10^1/4$ inches
120 pp
39 duotones,
20 b&w illustrations
$35

A monograph that explores Molinier's extraordinary life featuring an extensive collection of his formative collages, montage photographs, and objects of arousal. Texts in English and French. Smart Art Press/Plug In Editions

Manuel Ocampo
Heridas de la Lengua
September 1997

Softcover, $10^1/2$ x 11 inches
96 pp
64 color, 12 b&w illustrations
$30

This beautifully illustrated book documents one of the most important young artists to have emerged from Los Angeles in the last decade; his work updates the tradition of political allegorists like Gericault, Goya, Daumier and Golub.

SMART ART PRESS

2525 MICHIGAN AVENUE, BLDG. C1
SANTA MONICA, CA 90404
TEL. 310.264.4678   FAX 310.264.4682
www.smartartpress.com

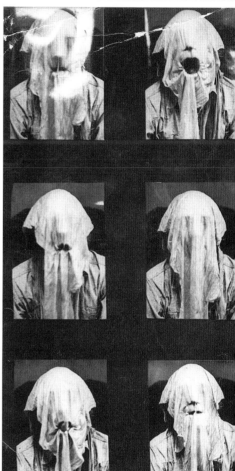

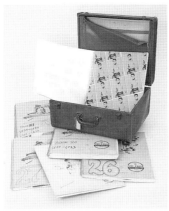

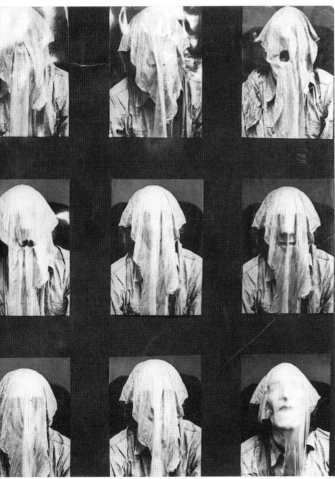

OPPOSITE PAGE
Top, middle and bottom left photos of Al Hansen, John Lennon, Andy Warhol, Yoko Ono by Valerie Herouvis.
Top left: Al Hansen in his Amsterdam suitcase. Photo: Valerie Herouvis.
Middle left and facing page: Al Hansen, Untitled photo grid, c.1970. Photos: Marion Morgenstern.
Bottom left and facing page: photo of Al Hansen by Valerie Herouvis.

THIS PAGE
Top left: to right: Traveling Suitcase, 1970-80s, mixed media, 28 x 17³/4 x 7⁷/8.”; Traveling Suitcase, 1970-80s, mixed media sketchbooks, 19¹/8 x 15³/4 x 9⁷/8”; Traveling Suitcase, 1970-80s, mixed media, 18¹/2 x 22 x 19¹/2.”
Top right: Al Hansen in his studio, Connecticut, c.1972. Photo: Valerie Herouvis.
Middle Right: Al Hansen just prior to the opening of the exhibition Köln Happening, Fluxus, 1970. Photo: Valerie Herouvis.

Al produced many significant works in Asolo, Italy at the studios of Francesco Conz. Archive Conz, Verona contains numerous objects, collages, assemblages. sculptures, texts, videotape and photographs by and of Al Hansen from 1970 to Al's death in 1995.